Guide to the
Electroni

Strategies to

Edited by

Steven Arnold

HIMSS Mission

To lead change in the healthcare information and management systems field through knowledge sharing, advocacy, collaboration, innovation, and community affiliations.

Printed in the U.S.A. 5 4 3 2 1

Requests for permission to reproduce any part of this work should be sent to:

Permissions Editor
HIMSS
230 E. Ohio St., Suite 500
Chicago, IL 60611-3270
nvitucci@himss.org

ISBN: 0-9761277-8-4

For more information about HIMSS, please visit www.himss.org.

About the Editor

Steven Arnold, MD, MS, MBA, CPE, is the President and CEO of Healthcare Consultants International. He specializes in Family Practice and holds a Master's degree in Clinical Psychology. His private practice of medicine was located in Beverly Hills, California, where he also founded and managed Entertainment Medical Specialists, Inc., a global organization catering to the entertainment industry. Dr. Arnold has more than 17 years of senior level healthcare experience and is a recognized consultant on healthcare quality, contracting, implementation of electronic health records, and the development of integrated delivery systems. He serves as a member of the HIMSS Enterprise Information Systems Steering Committee and the Advisory Board for the Katrina-Phoenix project. He co-chaired the Certification Commission for Health Information Technology's EHR Certification and Test Plan Committees.

In addition to his medical career, Dr. Arnold is a published author and poet, musician and composer, and is listed in several biographical editions.

Contributors

The following members of the HIMSS EHR Implementation Task Force contributed to the content and review of this book.

Roy A. Ackerman, PhD, EA
Technical Director
The Adjuvancy, LLC
Alexandria, Virginia

Vinod Aggarwal, MD, MS
Missouri City, Texas

Terri Andrews, RN, MBA
Clinical Systems Manager
Alamance Regional Medical Center
Burlington, North Carolina

**Cecilia A. Backman,
MBA, RRA, CPHQ**
Director of Consulting
Siemens
Malvern, Pennsylvania

Marge Benham-Hutchins, RN, MSN
Healthcare Informatics
Doctoral Student
Unversity of Arizona
College of Nursing
Euless, Texas

Lyle L. Berkowitz, MD
Medical Director, CIS
Northwestern Memorial
    Physicians Group
Chicago, Illinois

John Blandford
Vice President, Chief
    Information Officer
University Health System
San Antonio, Texas

Joseph A. Carr, CPHIMS
Chief Information Officer
New Jersey Hospital Association
Princeton, New Jersey

Yvonne Claudio, MS, PMP
Executive Director
National Association for Public
    Health Information Technology
Rockville, Maryland

Leo E. Cousineau, MD
Director of Medical Informatics
IMC
Reston, Virginia

Matthew Cowan
Vice President
Medical Software and
    Computer Systems, Inc.
Richmond, Virginia

Paul W. Durance, PhD
Director, IT
Huron Systems, Inc.
Twinsburg, Ohio

Larry Dux, CPHIMS, FHIMSS
Manager, Clinical
    Information Systems/PI
Community Memorial Hospital
Menomonee Falls, Wisconsin

Rosemary Ferdinand, RN, PhD
Deloitte Consulting LLP
National Life Science & Health Care
Summit, New Jersey

Christopher J. Flasco
Vice President, Professional Services
Noteworthy Medical Systems
Mayfield Heights, Ohio

**Susan P. Hanson, MBA,
    RHIA, FAHIMA**
TerraStar Consulting
Nashua, New Hampshire

Gary M. Klein, MD, MPH, MBA
Medical Director
KSK Consulting
Vienna, Virginia

Kathleen LePar, RN, MBA
Manager, Consulting Services
Beacon Partners, Inc.
Weymouth, Massachusetts

Donald L. Levick, MD,
MBA, CPHIMS
Physician Liaison
Information Services
President, Medical Staff
Lehigh Valley Hospital
Allentown, Pennsylvania

Kimberly S. Miller-Klein
Senior Manager
ECG Management Consultants, Inc.
Arlington, Virginia

Susan M. Moore
Manager
ECG Management Consultants, Inc.
Seattle, Washington

Stephanie Olivier, MBA, CPHIMS
Client Executive
Catholic Healthcare West IT
Phoenix, Arizona

Selina Pankovich
Montana Tech
Healthcare Informatics
Anaconda, Montana

Suniti Ponkshe
Associate Partner
Healthlink, a Division of IBM
McLean, Virginia

Beverly Power, MBA, PMP
Consultant
Database Management
Capabilities Project
San Leandro, California

Philip W. Rosen, MS
Principal
The Provider's Edge, LLC
Edison, New Jersey

Craig Rudlin, MD
Chair, Deployment Task Force
Med Software & Computer
Systems Inc.
Richmond, Virginia

Nanette Sayles, EdD,
RHIA, CCS, CHP
Program Director
Health Information
    Management & Technology
Macon State College
Macon, Georgia

Thomas F. Shubnell, PhD
Cardinal Consulting, Inc.
Plano, Texas

Cynthia Spurr, MBA, RN, C, FHIMSS
Corporate Director
Clinical Systems Management
Partners Healthcare System
Wellesley, Massachusetts

George Sullivan, MBA, CPHIMS
Director of Information
Technology Services
Mary Lanning Memorial Hospital
Hastings, Nebraska

Steven J. Woodson, MS
President
Medical Software &
    Computer Systems, Inc.
Richmond, Virginia

HIMSS Staff Liaison
Patricia Wise, RN, MSN, MA
Colonel, USA Ret'd
Vice President, Healthcare
Information Systems
HIMSS
Evans, Georgia

HIMSS Staff
Gail Arnett
Manager, Healthcare
Information Systems
HIMSS
Ann Arbor, Michigan

Contents

Introduction

*Diving into technology without an understanding of how it relates to
strategy and organizational and behavioral changes is like diving into
a swimming pool without filling it up first. It hurts if you
land on your head.*

POLITICAL PRESSURE BEGINS

From the President to the people: a national electronic health record
(EHR) system will become a reality in America. This is the mantra
that has become a bipartisan staple phrase in the nation's capital.
David Brailer, MD, PhD, former director of the Office of the National
Coordinator for Health Information Technology (ONC), echoed the
president's sentiments as he urged the development of public/private
coalitions for EHR adoption.

Supported by bipartisan EHR legislation, federal funding, and
Medicare involvement, EHR implementation is expected to reach at
least 50% penetration in fewer than 10 years.

EHR PENETRATION: A SLOW START

According to the American Medical Association (AMA), there were
813,770 physicians in the U.S. in 2000.[1] Forty-two percent (340,137)
practiced in a primary care setting. Further research from the Center
for Studying Health System Change (HSC) reveals that approximately
78% of all physicians practice in small groups of 8 physicians or less.[2]
Yet it is in the primary care setting where the majority of Americans
receive their healthcare. For this reason, this book focuses on implementing EHRs in small practices.

Estimates of the penetration of EHRs in the U.S. do not exceed 17%.[3] The Centers for Disease Control and Prevention (CDC) corroborates this statistic and suggests that healthcare lags significantly behind other industries in the adoption of information technology (IT). According to the CDC, only 8% of U.S. physicians use a computerized practitioner order entry system (CPOE), only 31% of hospital emergency departments use an EHR, and only 40% of emergency departments use automated drug dispensing systems.[4]

The majority of office-based physicians who have adopted EHRs practice in groups of more than 8 physicians. They include staff and group model HMO practices, followed by medical school faculty and large group practices.

By adding podiatrists (13,000), chiropractors (49,000), dentists (153,000), and optometrists (32,000)[5] to the number of healthcare providers in the country, the significance of failing to implement EHRs becomes even more critical. Although implementation of a public-private sector electronic health system in America is inevitable, the U.S. still trails far behind Australia, New Zealand, and the United Kingdom in deployment of EHRs.

According to the *Connecting for Health Report*, it will take 7 to 10 years to achieve wide-scale adoption of EHRs across the U.S. at a total cost of $21.6 billion to $43.2 billion.[6] Fortunately, the cost pales in comparison to the return on investment that advanced clinical IT will bring to the U.S. health system.

One need not look far outside the healthcare industry to understand that IT implementation is, at best, difficult to achieve. In 1995, U.S. government and businesses spent approximately $81 billion on software projects that were eventually canceled and an additional $59 billion for projects that ran over budget. Nearly one-third of all IT projects were cancelled and only one-sixth of all projects were completed on time and within budget.[7] Reasons for failure abound, but common factors are present in many of these ill-fated ventures. These include failure to research the project before implementation, a lack of executive support, under-budgeting, failure to integrate the IT concept with the business strategy, failure to achieve buy-in from users, lack of in-house skills and experience with IT systems, failure to change the structure and culture of the organization to accept IT integration, and failure to build a project team to manage the entire process.

If IT implementation fails so often outside of healthcare where companies may be better organized and funded, is it any wonder that the task of implementing a national system of interoperable EHR systems appears so daunting?

This challenge must be met if we are to achieve the level of quality and safety of healthcare that Americans deserve. Therefore, it must be done. It can be done. It will be done.

Several themes overlap in this book by design. These include attainment of support, alignment of resources, managing change, dealing with external forces that impose change, meeting challenges to implementation, and avoiding risks and pitfalls. These themes are stressed multiple times, for without successful completion of each task, EHR implementation will fail.

The healthcare industry cannot view EHRs merely as a means of achieving better efficiency. The EHR must be viewed as a means of achieving its mission: to improve the delivery of coordinated quality healthcare, promote preventive care, and avoid errors. It must, above all, help caregivers to "do no harm." Finally, it must integrate data into a set of useful information that can be acted upon for the sake of patients.

CHAPTER 1

Electronic Health Records Defined

RESPONSE TO EVOLUTION

To appreciate the need for, and to define the features and characteristics of an electronic health record (EHR), we first need to recognize how the practice of medicine has evolved:

1. From the treatment of acute illness, to the prevention of disease;
2. From considering each patient as an isolated entity, the sole focus and point of care, to perceiving the patient as a member of a population; and
3. From a focus on the individual, to the broader perspective of public health.

The EHR must address and facilitate this continued evolution.

Historically, emphasis has been placed on an individual patient's acute illness. Physicians were taught to document an encounter through what has been termed a 'SOAP' format (subjective, objective, assessment, and plan). Early attempts to computerize medical records tried to follow this format and, thus merely produced an electronic version of the written record. The disadvantage inherent in this process is that it focuses the physician on each episode of individual patient care and not on longitudinal, integrative care for both individual patients and the population as a whole.

Medicine is shifting its focus away from viewing the patient as an isolated entity and toward perceiving the patient as part of a population. Critical information about a patient's individual disease can be found in a population's genetic fabric and the way that the environment affects it. For example, the patient's family genetics may influence the risks for developing breast and colon cancers. The environment may further affect those risks through cigarette smoking and malnutrition.

PUBLIC HEALTH AND CONSUMER CARE

The SOAP format does not address the fact that medicine is evolving from an individual patient perspective to the broader concept of public health. Physicians must think beyond the acute illness to disease prevention and embrace the more global aspect of public health.

As medicine evolves, so must the EHR. The EHR should be able to share information between physicians and public health organizations. Immunization rates and communicable diseases are only two of the many factors that could adversely affect large populations of patients. Indeed, an effective EHR must help medicine to evolve. It must improve documentation, implement standards of care, and longitudinally monitor compliance with those standards.

There are at least four components of this perspective that can be greatly enhanced by the adoption of EHR:

1. *Communicable diseases:* The patient's lifestyle may define risks for a communicable disease and the probability that the patient will infect others. An effective EHR must be able to record information relating to infectious disease and confidentially report them to departments of health.

2. *Disease entities:* One disease may impact another. Obesity, for example, may lead to diabetes in a genetically-predisposed individual. Diabetes, in turn, is a leading cause of heart disease, strokes, and death. The underlying pathology (obesity) is rooted in societal behavior and hence requires addressing societal (population) issues as well as the needs of the individual patient. The EHR should be capable of collecting data on the prevalence of obesity, its associated co-morbidities, and successful outcomes from therapy. This

information can be made available to public health agencies to help them develop, refine, and validate public policy. The EHR should also identify those patients who could benefit from participation in clinical trials or from specific treatment protocols and medications.

3. *The patient as a consumer of healthcare resources:* A patient's health financially impacts the entire population and, ultimately, the national budget. A long-term goal to controlling escalating healthcare costs is to limit the need for healthcare by faithfully promoting preventive healthcare to every patient. An EHR system must, therefore, promote preventive care as well as the management of active diseases.

4. *The individual as a member of society:* An individual disabled by disease may no longer be able to earn wages, support his family, or be a "productive" member of society. Again, EHR promotion of preventive health and better management of disease is imperative in lowering the cost to society at large.

As medicine continues to evolve from patient-centric to population-centric, the EHR must serve as a conduit of information between the clinician and public health organizations. Based upon patient data collected in physician's offices, the EHR can create a feedback loop with collected population data being reported back to the office-based clinicians.

OFFICE-BASED CONSUMER CARE

On a more secular level, the office-based clinical practice has also evolved. This evolution has been driven by three major factors:

1. The rise and control of third party payors;
2. The publication of national standards of care based on evidence of therapeutic efficacy collected from large clinical trials and surveillance of large populations; and
3. Malpractice litigation.

Office-based clinicians are urged to do the following:

• Improve their documentation into the patient's medical record. Medical records must be legible, complete and clear.

• Adopt national standards of care for disease management and apply these standards uniformly to every patient. Unnecessary deviation from the mean is less tolerated.

- Monitor patient compliance with the recommended therapies resulting from these standards.

The EHR must, therefore, provide a framework that facilitates compliance with, and implementation of, these office-based components.

EVOLUTION: FROM PAPER TO ELECTRONICS

Until the Industrial Revolution made it possible for patients to travel beyond the confines of their small towns, physicians knew each patient personally. Physicians typically practiced alone, and there was little need to communicate an individual's medical history with anyone else. As small towns grew larger and more than a single physician served the population, it became more important to record a person's medical history. The paper chart filled this need but was fraught with problems such as a lack of standards, inadequate documentation, and illegible handwriting. The SOAP format was created to standardize both patient care and its documentation.

The first generation of electronic *medical* records (EMRs) merely duplicated paper records. Although they improved legibility, they offered few other improvements.

The second generation of EMR added the concept of *summaries*: simple lists of the patient's diseases and treatments prescribed. However, they failed to describe the patient's overall health and follow it from disease to prevention of disease.

The third generation of EMR added a *longitudinal perspective* to the medical history that permitted the physician to detect trends in a patient's illness. However, they were still organized by acute illnesses and did not adequately address future disease and preventive health. Most EMRs sold today are third-generation systems.

Electronic *health* records transcend EMRs, evolving into a fourth-generation system that addresses the needs of all stakeholders including clinicians, patients, and the public health system.

EHRs provide dual perspectives (both acute and longitudinal) of the patient's medical history in order to identify early signs of illness. They implement standards of care and monitor compliance with those standards, promote preventive care, warn of potential adverse therapeutic interactions and duplication of therapy, identify noncompliant patients, proactively address disease management, and provide a means to establish communication with public health systems.

PERSONAL HEALTH RECORDS (PHR)

There is an important distinction between a *personal* health record and an *electronic* health record. The PHR is a chronological listing of illnesses, hospitalizations, surgeries, and medications. It is a statement of fact. In contrast, the EHR is both a statement of fact and an interpretation of that fact; diagnoses are derived from combinations of physical and diagnostic information.

Understanding the difference between EHRs and PHRs is critical to implementing regional health information organizations (RHIOs) or a single national health network. It is also paramount to deciding how patients should be able to access their own medical records within those networks.

The PHR resides with the patient. As the sole guardian of the PHR, the patient would be liable for any medical errors resulting from editing the record.

In contrast, the relationship between ownership and custody of the EHR is not as clear. Debate over who actually owns the records has created legal rifts between the stakeholders. Because the EHR resides with the clinician, the ability to enter information into the record historically has been said to be the purview of those caregivers. Patients have argued, however, that ownership of the EHR belongs to them and that they, therefore, have the right to unrestricted access to that record.

Legal representatives argue that the patient not only has the right to read but to edit the record as well. Physicians, however, argue that unfiltered information, including unreviewed lab tests and the clinician's subjective comments, may harm the patient. For example, a patient who is able to review an electronically captured lab error before the physician is able to correct it may be unduly worried by the experience. Moreover, deletion of important documented information by the patient, including drug allergies, may be detrimental to that patient. Such altered records may be viewed by other clinicians who may then deliver the wrong medication as a result of the missing data.

Direct patient access to the EHR raises issues of liability for both the clinician and patient. Maintaining confidentiality is of paramount importance, but the debate over what can or cannot be edited will continue until legal rights are solidified.

CHAPTER 2

Driving EHR Implementation

EXTERNAL FORCES

Political

There has been increasing federal support for EHRs since 2003. This is likely due to the government's recognition that healthcare needs to incorporate information technologies if it is to rein in near double-digit growth in annual spending, reduce avoidable medical errors, and improve the health and well-being of Americans.

President Bush became the first president to mention EHR systems in his State of the Union Address when he called for the computerization of health records to avoid medical errors, reduce costs and improve care. He called for the majority of Americans to have interoperable EHRs within 10 years and signed an Executive Order establishing the position of the National Coordinator for Health Information Technology. Shortly after his appointment to this post, Dr. David Brailer created a framework for strategic action to guide nationwide adoption of health information technology in both the public and private sectors.[8]

Promoting EHRs has gained bipartisan support in Congress and, under the Bush Administration, Mark McClellan, Administrator for

CMS, has focused Medicare on providing financial incentives for physicians who implement EHRs.

The political pressure to implement EHRs is merely a response to the economic, public health and societal issues that have arisen over the last several decades.

Economic

U.S. healthcare spending increased for the sixth straight year in a row, hitting $1.44 trillion in 2003, a 9.3% increase over the 2001 expenditure. This cost translates into an average expenditure of $5,440 per person, up $419 from $5,021 in 2001.[9]

Healthcare spending grew 5.7 percentage points faster than the overall U.S. economy, as measured by the growth of the gross domestic product (GDP). This represents a growth in the share of GDP devoted to healthcare from 13.3% in 2000 to 14.9% in 2002.

Despite the annual expenditure of $1.44 trillion for healthcare in the U.S., the system is still plagued with inefficiency and poor quality. These wasted costs are passed on to the purchasers of healthcare, including employers, the federal government, and/or patients themselves.

The Rand Institute suggests that annual savings from a national EHR system could reach $162 billion per year.[10] Nearly half of that savings, $77 billion, can derive from improved efficiencies, reductions in duplication of tests, reducing preventable medical errors, and improved administration. The rest of the savings will be derived from lower death rates, fewer medical complications and fewer employee sick days from chronic diseases. The precise cost from preventable illness or complications of chronic disease is unknown but the cost of diabetes alone was estimated to be $91.8 billion in 2002.[11]

Based on a total projected cost between $21.6 billion to $43.2 billion to implement a nationwide EHR and maintenance costs of $10 billion per year, the total cost is easily covered by the savings after the first year.

Public Health

Congressman Patrick Kennedy (D-RI) has suggested that "...as many as 98,000 Americans die in hospitals every year as a result of medical errors…and countless more are injured," and that "…45% of the time, providers fail to deliver scientifically accepted care."[12] A nationally-linked EHR system can significantly improve these sobering statistics because EHRs allow feedback of clinical data to public health entities to help guide them in designing and implementing regulations and standards of care.

The Blue Cross/Blue Shield Association (BCBSA), as a member of the National Alliance for Healthcare Information Technology (the Alliance), has committed to encouraging the implementation of information technology to improve care and patient safety and to promote the use of evidence-based medicine. Various BCBSA plans have already begun to promote information technology by communicating critical patient data between healthcare providers. They are also funding electronic networks that will connect doctors, hospitals, insurers, and patients. By doing so, the BCBSA believes it will demonstrate cost-benefits and increase collaboration among all parties. Because the BCBSA plans insure more than 88 million Americans, they are positioned to play a dominant role in influencing the use of EHRs in ambulatory and hospital settings and in determining the way EHRs will be used in the provision of and payment for healthcare in the future.

Societal

Patients today are not the same patients of their parents' generation. Societal changes have produced dramatic shifts in the way consumers make healthcare decisions and in the sources of information they rely upon in reaching those decisions. A 2002 nationwide survey of almost 20,000 households found that the percentage of consumers who said they would follow their doctor's recommendation without question had fallen from 53% in 2000 to only 36% in 2002.[13] The rise in the use of the Internet has had a significant impact in this reduction. Patients sometimes arrive at their physicians' offices brandishing healthcare articles that they feel are relevant to their situations. A major challenge for clinicians, therefore, is to provide reliable sources of information that are medically sound and truly relevant to their patients' particular healthcare needs.

EHRs provide a mechanism to extend the traditional physician-patient relationship. For example, an EHR might provide the following capabilities:

- For patients to receive a copy of their test results electronically along with interpretive information;
- To create a Web site with quality medical references and health maintenance guidelines;
- To facilitate communications between physicians and their patients by secure e-mail; and
- To send reminders for preventive care at appropriate intervals.

All of these capabilities require a new approach to the delivery of medicine, made necessary by the increasingly demanding expectations from patients.

Unfortunately, it does not appear that the general public is aware of the EHR concept or of the government's drive to build a national system. In a recent Harris Poll telephone survey, 1,012 adults aged 18 or older were asked a series of questions relating to their understanding of EHRs.[14] Of these respondents, only 29% were aware of the call for a nationwide system and 71% were not. On a scale of "not concerned at all" to "very concerned," 42% were "very concerned" about the possibility of sharing of their medical information without their permission, and 38% were very concerned that sensitive personal medical-record information might be leaked because of weak security. On a scale of "very low" to "high," a total of 56% had "high" concern about privacy. Finally, when it came to the importance of patients being able to track their own personal healthcare information, 82% felt that it was "somewhat" (37%) to "very" (45%) important.

HIPAA and Security Issues

The growth of EHRs and the linking of clinical databases have produced growing concern regarding the privacy and security of health information, even while enhancing the ability of healthcare providers to access clinically relevant health information. Many fear that transporting such information over the emerging national information infrastructure will result in greater vulnerability to the patient's privacy. Concerns are escalating because more sensitive information (e.g., HIV status, psychiatric records, and genetic information) is now stored in EMRs. If we are to reap the positive benefits of EHRs, we must first define these concerns and offer suggestions for mitigating the risks.

Addressing these concerns requires both becoming aware of the vulnerabilities that exist in EHRs and defining various means for protecting such information.

Concerns over the privacy and security of EHRs fall into two broad categories:

1. Concerns about improper releases of information; and
2. Concerns about improper access to patient records.

Inappropriate release of confidential information can occur whenever users within the organization access or disseminate information in violation of HIPAA guidelines. An outsider who breaks into an organization's computer system also imposes an obvious threat to the EHR. Therefore, organizational threats could assume many forms. Once the organization identifies the unique risks, however, various system controls can be implemented to mitigate these threats.

As confidential information flows among healthcare organizations, health plans, business associates, and other healthcare entities, inadvertent disclosure of health information may occur without the patient's knowledge. These concerns are intensified by computer networking that permits rapid, large-scale, and potentially unobserved access to data.

The challenge for EHRs is to achieve a balance between protecting patient information and providing caregivers access to the information required for patient care. At a minimum, security policies need to be developed that include "need to know" access, and all users must sign a statement of acceptance and compliance with these policies.

The EHR system must adhere to HIPAA requirements. The EHR must contain a field to identify whether a patient permits the exchange of his/her medical record. An audit trail can then identify anyone who has accessed the patient's medical record. In addition, EHRs must be able to grant and remove a user's access.

HIPAA may require limited access to parts of the medical record based on the user's role in the medical office. However, this may not be feasible in the small-to-medium practice setting. For example, the appointment secretary may indeed need to know the patient's diagnosis so that adequate time and appropriate supplies or equipment can be scheduled for the next patient visit. Similarly, the bookkeeper may need to review the medical record in order to correctly complete ICD-9 and CPT coding for submission to Medicare.

INTERNAL FORCES

It is not only forces external to medical practices that affect EHRs. In addition to political and government pressures, societal forces, economic changes, and technology, factors inside the practice also drive them toward change. These include financial changes, practice liability, and incentives to improve performance.

Economic

Despite the fact that medical practices supply services to their communities, they are not immune from the fundamental economic pressures that affect other service organizations. Like any organization, medical practices must offset the ever-rising costs of doing business. However, unlike organizations such as shipping companies or accounting firms, small- and medium-sized physician practices are barred from passing on rising costs (e.g., malpractice premiums) to their customers. In the absence of higher fees, these practices must maximize efficiency to control expenditures. Failure to do so can make the costs of providing these crucial services prohibitive; when a practice is no longer economically viable, society as a whole pays the price.

The most obvious economic benefit of EHRs is the potential for increased efficiency. A well-designed implementation can easily reduce the personnel needed for creating and maintaining proper documentation. In addition to these obligatory costs, physicians are increasingly called upon to engage in activities that, while time-consuming, are usually not reimbursable. These activities include telephone consultations, medication renewals, and notification of lab results. An EHR that addresses these tasks through automation can greatly improve the economic viability of the practice.

Increased efficiency not only affects a practice's expenditures but its potential revenues as well. Automation can ease the clinician's documentation burden, and the ability to report data can trigger higher reimbursement (pay for performance) by third-party payors. Claims once rejected for insufficient documentation rarely occur when submitted through an EHR. Finally, automating tasks such as appointment scheduling, lab ordering and entry, and prescribing can have an enormous impact on the efficiency and income of a practice.

Liability

When considering the cost of providing medical services, medical liability and malpractice insurance loom in the forefront. Because of the rate of litigation and the growing size of settlements and damages, these expenses are rising more rapidly than reimbursement in almost every state. Some physicians have left practice because they can no longer obtain affordable insurance. Documentation is at the root of many of these cases: most are lost by the physician as a result of poor record keeping (thereby offering limited legal options) or by the commission of errors secondary to inadequate documentation. Improved documentation alone has the potential to annually save billions of dollars and, more importantly, thousands of lives.

Incentives

As important as these benefits may be to a practice from a business perspective, they are only some of the potential advantages. Complete and detailed automated documentation can reduce the risk of adverse drug interactions, apply standards of care to disease management, and promote preventive health. EHRs can also facilitate communication between the patient and physician, thus promoting health education. Recognizing the benefits of EHR, Medicare and several third-party payors have joined the drive to promote pay for performance through the use of information technology.

EFFICIENCY

In summary, EHRs can bring many advantages to medical practices. These include:
1. Decreasing the time required to completely document a patient encounter, thereby permitting more time for clinician/patient interaction.
2. Providing complete documentation necessary to "justify" third party reimbursement.

3. Improving the quality of care by providing notification of potential drug interactions and national standards of care.
4. Decreasing the time required to review laboratory results, approve prescription refill requests and other non-reimbursable chores.
5. Improving communications between clinicians and patients to promote patient education and improve satisfaction.
6. Decreasing the risk for medical liability by improving documentation and reducing errors of omission and commission.

Although EHRs can certainly be a positive force on medical practice, they are not without cost. This will be explored further in the next chapter.

CHAPTER 3

Costs and Benefits

The return on investment (ROI) is the major impetus for implementing an EHR. It is critical to recognize that the ROI consists of easily measured (concrete) costs and benefits, as well as more abstract benefits that are difficult to quantify in terms of dollars, but are perhaps even more valuable in terms of patient care and the quality of life for staff.

It is also important to recognize that there are costs associated with not implementing an EHR, and these must be factored into the equation when calculating the ROI. The costs associated with not implementing an EHR derive from errors of omissions and commissions with respect to care of the patient (and the medical record).

In most cases, the costs and benefits are obvious or intuitive once the concept of an EHR is understood. Therefore, rather than belabor the point, the following is a synopsis of the costs and benefits that together equate to the ROI associated with implementing an EHR (Table 3-1).

The bottom line is simply this: EHR is extremely cost effective and has a large (positive) ROI that clearly justifies the initial expense both in terms of cost of the hardware and software, and the stress and effort involved in implementation.

Table 3-1: Costs and Benefits of an EHR

I. Costs of Implementing an EHR

Concrete (easily as signed dollar value)	Software
	Hardware
	Support (on-going)
	Decreased productivity (temporary during transition from paper)
	Increased labor costs (temporary)
Abstract (dollar value not readily assigned)	Stress on staff during implementation

II. Costs of Not Implementing an EHR

Errors of omission	**1. Medical liability for poor documentation**
	a. Failure to provide immunizations
	b. Failure to adequately notify patients of medication recalls or new meds
	c. Failure to screen or otherwise treat family members with familial disease
	d. Failure to provide preventive care
	e. Medication errors from not providing patient educational material
	f. Poor documentation of extra office contacts and telephone contacts
	g. Poor communication regarding labs, etc.
	2. Increased risk of failing to meet regulatory requirements, licensing, and requirements of state and federal law
	a. Failure to report communicable diseases or immunizations
	b. Failure to identify patients eligible for clinical studies
	c. Poor documentation for Medicaid, Medicare and other third party audits
	d. Failure to adequately document diagnoses and therapies for medication audits
	3. Missed opportunity for increased reimbursement
	a. Loss of incentive pay when preventive care is not provided
	b. Inadequate documentation of ICD-9 and CPT codes

Errors of commission	1. Increased liability
	a. Drug interactions: drug-drug, drug allergy and drug-diagnosis
	b. Failure to diagnose due to poor documentation or organization of the medical record
	c. Failure to follow up to determine efficacy of therapy
	d. Medication errors due to poor legibility, confusing names, etc.
	2. Decreased reimbursement
	a. Failure to adhere to national standards of care, leading to loss of incentive payments
	3. Increased cost to patients
	a. Failure to adhere to formularies
	4. Decreased quality of medical care
	a. Failure to adhere to national standards of care
	b. Failure to follow up to determine efficacy of therapy
	c. Failure to diagnose due to poor documentation or organization
	d. Failure to recognize drug interactions

III. Benefits of Implementing an EHR

Concrete	Increased revenue from pay for performance
	Increased revenue from recalls and patient follow-up
	Decreased labor costs
	Increased productivity of clinicians and staff
	Decreased medical and regulatory liability
Abstract	Less time spent reviewing lab results, calling patients, refilling prescriptions, answering telephone calls, etc.; ability to spend more time away from office
	Greater satisfaction in practicing preventive healthcare
	Less time spent on tedious paperwork and redundant communications
	Improved quality of life

The practice must realize and accept that many of the costs/benefits of an EHR may not be immediately realized.

Third party payors will also accrue savings when their participating practices have EHRs. These savings derive from automated chart reviews and audits, adherence to national standards, and preventive care (which lowers long term costs and increases the third party's competitiveness in the market and patient loyalty), and help retain patients long enough for the third party to reap benefits of decreased medical costs. These savings justify third party contribution toward the cost of EHRs.

CHAPTER 4

Addressing the Unique Nature of Small Individual and Group Practices

Seventy-eight percent of all physicians in the U.S. practice in small groups of eight physicians or fewer.[2,15] It is here where the majority of Americans receive their healthcare, and for this reason, this book focuses on these ambulatory medical practices.

Carol Diamond, MD, Managing Director at the Markle Foundation and Chair of Connecting for Health, said:

> *"Electronic health records have the potential to help reduce medical errors, lower costs and empower patients. However, without the widespread adoption of electronic health records by small and medium physician practices—that represent more than half of the practices in this country—and the requirements for achieving the level of interconnectivity necessary to allow for the effective exchange of health related information, the benefits of information technology cannot be fully realized."[16]*

These facts and remarks highlight the profound necessity for implementing EHRs in smaller, private practices across the nation.

Unfortunately, most EHR vendors focus sales on large healthcare organizations (e.g., hospitals and large clinic centers).

The lack of attention given to smaller practices may be the result of higher costs to market and to implement EHR systems. There is no formula that can be universally applied to such large numbers of geographically isolated and diverse practices. There are, however, several guiding principles and strategies that can help shepherd these practices through an EHR implementation. These principles will be addressed in the chapters that follow.

SMEs VERSUS LARGER ENTERPRISES

Small- to medium-sized enterprises (SMEs) tend to be flexible organizations with a simple structure and power culture; the person at the top typically calls the shots. There are very few layers of bureaucracy—the senior decision maker is often the IT champion, so a top-down approach to getting anything done (e.g., an EHR implementation) is not usually resisted, and overt buy-in is as easy as saying "do it." If the decisions are on the mark, the organization flourishes; if they are not, the organization flounders. With appropriate leadership, an SME can quickly adapt to its environment, as it is often free of the red tape that hinders larger organizations.

If the healthcare SME is large enough to have an office manager, certain decisions may migrate from the physician leadership to the manager. In this case, the office manager may become the IT champion, although he/she typically will require the physicians' approval and support. If the physician leader is also the IT champion, but the office manager is not on board, then IT implementation may come to a grinding halt.

SMEs are driven by a quest for efficiency and not by a competitive desire to tip the market scales in their favor. Unlike large hospital chains and clinics, where there is a desire to increase market share, most individual healthcare providers do not see business growth as a priority. Rather, their priority is to improve efficiency to a level of cost-effective management and profitability. They seek a reduction in workload—one that is already in "maximum overdrive"—and desire a better lifestyle as a result. Healthcare SMEs, therefore, introduce technology to control and to manage operational activities. They do not think terms of sustainable competitive advantage, competitive strategy, or about how technology fits into their business mission. In most cases they have no business mission other than to take care of patients. However, even to do this successfully, they may have to alter the structure and even the organization of the business prior to the introduction of technology.

When implementing an EHR in an SME, the implementation leader or leadership team must be careful not to apply methods typical of large healthcare organizations to their small, private-practice environment. Trying to apply large-scale implementation methods to smaller organizations is not only ineffective but can be disastrous. Large-scale methods may not address the peculiar needs and personalities inherent in smaller practices.

This point also applies to governmental agencies and their desire to roll out a national enterprise system of EHRs. Interoperable standards must be created so that different systems can "talk" with one another. But even after these standards have been implemented, it is still not practical to think that implementation in the public sector will translate easily to smaller medical practices. Modifications may be necessary to accommodate the nature of small practices' operations. Only when their disparate needs are met will SMEs be able to join the drive toward national implementation of EHRs.

CHAPTER 5

The Importance of Stakeholders

ARE STAKEHOLDERS IMPORTANT?

It is not safe to consider an EHR implementation if you have not considered the needs of all of your stakeholders. Stakeholders are people or organizations with a vested interest in the outcome of the project. They need not be direct stakeholders who have invested financial resources into the EHR implementation. They can be any individual or entity whom your implementation will affect in any way, either directly or indirectly.

If you work in a small medical practice and believe that you have either one stakeholder or just a few stakeholders who share the same ideals, objectives, and processes to achieve them, start worrying. You have either miscounted or have not done enough homework to determine what your stakeholders want.

For example, even if you work in a two-physician office, you may have more stakeholders than you realize. These include, but are not limited to, the following:

1. *Yourself*: The greatest stakeholder of all, the one who benefits the most if things go well and who suffers most if they do not.
2. *Patients*: Clearly the ones who stand to benefit from a successful EHR implementation in the form of improved delivery of health-

care. Patients may be connected electronically to the practice to schedule appointments and to communicate with the clinicians and office staff.

3. *Staff*: No financial investment in EHR here, but there must be a commitment to make it work. If your staff feels that EHR systems will negatively affect their jobs, the barriers they build can be insurmountable.

4. *Hospitals*: Critical patient information needs to be exchanged between the practice and the hospital.

5. *Payors*: Point of service improvement in healthcare can reduce unnecessary costs for a health plan and improve return on investment (ROI) through pay for performance.

6. *Uncle Sam*: A national system of EHRs tied together to make healthcare information portable is in the nation's best interest. Uncle Sam may also provide financial incentives to hasten EHR implementation. Direct communication (interoperability) between medical practices and public health (e.g., immunization and communicable disease registries) is vital to a national system of preventive health.

7. *Local Governments*: Especially those local governments that have set up immunization registries can benefit from improved collection of data and population management.

8. *Employers*: Some, like those in the Leapfrog Group, may also be payors. It is, therefore, in their best interest to keep employees safe and healthy, and reduce cost.

9. *Insurers*: Medical malpractice carriers may be encouraged to offer premium discounts to practices that implement EHRs.

10. *Vendors*: Medical practice satisfaction with the system represents future growth to those companies.

The needs of these many stakeholders often conflict with each other. Patients as stakeholders may want access to their files in order to alter what you have written in their record. As a clinician you may find this potentially detrimental to your patient if essential information is missing, such as drug allergies. This information may be required at a critical time during a medical emergency. For example, without a medication history, an unconscious trauma victim may be given an injection to which he is allergic.

If this seems complicated at the level of the medical practice, it becomes even more complex with a national EHR initiative! For example, once a certification process is enacted for EHR systems, different stakeholders may come into conflict. Payors may want the certification process to be as comprehensive and as detailed as possible. Vendors, however, may not want to invest more money into a system that is not quite as comprehensive but works well in most physicians' offices. Government agencies, such as CMS, may want patients to have electronic access to their records. Physicians, however, may balk at providing that access. The federal government may want every man, woman, and child in America to have their healthcare information shared with every authorized user. The American Civil Liberties Union (ACLU), however, may sue to limit that potential breach in patient confidentiality.

STAKEHOLDERS IN THE MEDICAL PRACTICE SETTING

The primary stakeholders in an EHR implementation in a medical practice include (a) executives and/or practice managers; (b) physicians who use the system; (c) ancillary personnel supporting the physician; (d) secretarial and other office staff; and (e) information technology personnel or software vendors who support the EHR from a technical perspective. All of these stakeholders have to work towards a common vision to achieve an effective EHR. This type of project requires that clinicians drive the project, but the supporting information technology and ancillary staff are critical in the EHR implementation. Each stakeholder has a different role and responsibility within the project, as defined below.

ROLES AND RESPONSIBILITIES OF STAKEHOLDERS IN THE PRACTICE

Executive, or Practice Manager

In a small group practice, the executive or manager is either an office manager or one of the physicians in the group. In a solo practice without an office manager, the choice is obvious. Although all administrative personnel should support the EHR initiative, only one individual should be designated to serve as the executive sponsor. This executive sponsor must possess the authority, either through legitimate, expert, or referent power, to ensure that the implementation will not only commence but progress through every milestone.

Leading the project, however, is not enough. The sponsor will also need to remove roadblocks and assure adequate funding. He/she must also act as a change agent; without such a leader, necessary changes in the practice's structure and workflows will either not occur or will be suboptimal.

It is important to remind the reader that migration to an EHR is not about technology. It is about re-engineering how the practice functions. Technology may serve as an enabler, but the critical mission is to change the way clinicians perform their work.

Physicians and Other Clinicians

Clinicians play a pivotal role in an EHR implementation's success. This category of caregivers can include physicians, nurses, nurse practitioners, physician assistants, nutritionists, psychologists, physical therapists, and any other ancillary personnel working directly with patients.

The clinician's primary responsibility occurs in the design phase when the content of the health record must be decided. This includes the development of content for problem lists, progress notes, procedure notes, consultations, lab orders and results, patient prescriptions, patient education, and follow-up instructions. Physicians need to define the rules that will trigger clinical decision support. Furthermore, workflows must be carefully designed to facilitate execution of an appropriate electronic plan of care.

Clinicians also need to determine how information will be generated, accessed, viewed and maintained. When developing content, clinicians need to meld both their own clinical experience and national evidence-based medicine guidelines into the system.

Finally, because different specialties may have different needs, it is important to design an EHR system in one of two ways. The first is to produce a common data set that all physicians will use and then customize that data to specialty-specific information. The second is to build or buy a specialty-specific EHR that is interoperable with other EHR systems.

Administrative, Accounting, and Other Office Staff

Receptionists, appointment secretaries, and bookkeepers are major users of the information compiled in an EHR. When designing a system, consider how the staff will use information such as patient demographics and insurance data within the office. Determine how inter-office messages will be sent to and from the clinicians, and structure the process for relaying information to outside entities such as third party payors and regulatory agencies.

Information Technology Personnel

The typical SME has neither an IT department nor a dedicated IT professional. Yet even a solo medical practice needs someone to maneuver the implementation through all the technology hurdles. Hardware and software must be correctly installed and maintained. New staff must be trained. Established staff may need to be retrained, especially whenever upgrades to the software are distributed by the vendor. In most cases an outside consultant or vendor should be engaged to fulfill this crucial role.

CHAPTER 6

The Ten Phases of Implementation

EHR selection and implementation remains a complicated and somewhat uncertain proposition. In fact, the challenge is significant enough to discourage many organizations, especially small practices, from implementing an EHR. Therefore, great care must be taken when selecting an EHR system and must begin long before the first sales representative comes through your door.

EARLY CHALLENGES: BARRIERS

In the early stages of project planning, barriers relate to the following:
1. Lack of administrative support or buy-in;
2. Failure to communicate the vision;
3. Failure to manage stakeholder expectations; and
4. Lack of financial and employee resources, skills and experience.

As the planning proceeds additional barriers are likely to emerge, including:
1. Failure to implement adequate access controls and compliance with HIPAA security and privacy laws; and

2. Inability to establish interoperability between other systems including lab, pharmacy, public health, and legacy systems within the same office.

Once implementation begins there will be other barriers such as:

1. Failure to incorporate the designed changes into the structure and workflow of the practice;
2. Failure to allot enough time and effort to support the implementation;
3. Failure to manage, at least temporarily, a dual system of paper and electronic records; and
4. Failure to integrate the EHR across the full scope of functions and services implicit to patient care.

Therefore, it is important to separate EHR implementation into phases so that these barriers can be identified, addressed, and overcome.

EHR IMPLEMENTATION PHASES

The first step in the EHR implementation process is the development of an EHR strategy. That strategy must meet the needs of the medical practice from the delivery of quality patient care to its profitability as a business. Managing the transition—the change in how things are accomplished— must be an integral part of the strategy.

The ten phases of EHR implementation are outlined below and discussed in detail in the following chapters.

Phase 1: Achieving Buy-In
- Stakeholders
- EHR champion(s)

Phase 2: Analysis
- Business needs and mission
- Practice assessment
- Identification and analysis of processes
- Identification of resource requirements
- Identification of technology needs
- Identification of barriers

Phase 3: Design
- Assess readiness to go electronic
- Analyze and redesign workflows
- Project planning

Phase 4: Managing Change
- Process change
- Planned versus emergent change
- Managing change
- Identify and overcoming resistance

Phase 5: Selection and Procurement
- Technology
- Interface development
- Security and system access
- Reporting
- Clinical content
- Customization
- Paper versus digital records
- Data conversion
- Maintenance
- Disaster planning

Phase 6: Installation and Set-Up
- Human activity systems
- Vision and communication
- Managing dual record systems simultaneously
- Transition planning
- "Big bang" versus incremental change

Phase 7: Training
- Train all users
- Evaluate, on an ongoing basis, staff's performance and retrain/coach as needed

Phase 8: Go-Live
- Pilot the system
- Expand to full implementation
- Plan for contingencies

Phase 9: Maintenance and Support

- Arrange for help for all issues (e.g., user questions, repair, outages, new installations) with dispatch capabilities. Match the hours of coverage to the office's schedule
- Arrange for routine daily maintenance (e.g., backups, preventive maintenance)
- Disaster recovery
- Continuing to manage change

Phase 10: Post-Implementation

- Develop strategies to increase clinical trial revenue using the new EHR capabilities
- Develop strategies to increase revenue for pay for performance
- Mine clinical data (e.g., identify treatment efficacy or disease prevalence)
- Mine business data (e.g., target revenue by patient demographics, insurance reimbursement, plan types, referring practices/facilities, procedures)
- Develop and institute best medical practices on an ongoing basis
- Implement enhancements to the system when available

The ultimate vision for the integrated electronic medical practice is to have seamless interoperability between all offices of the practice and with electronic systems at affiliated hospitals, clinics, laboratories, and the like. This holistic environment produces an up-to-date, accurate, and complete clinical picture of the patient that enables the best quality care to be provided, regardless of where the patient is treated. It also allows the business side of the practice to run in a more efficient and profitable manner. However, the ultimate goal of complete interoperability awaits national standards for communicating data between disparate healthcare systems.

CHAPTER 7

Phase 1: Achieving Buy-In

ACHIEVING AND MAINTAINING STAKEHOLDER BUY-IN

No EHR implementation can be successful without stakeholder support and approval, or buy-in, at the beginning of a project. It is equally important to foster continued involvement and support from the stakeholders throughout the implementation. Feedback, including performance measurements and milestone achievements, must be provided to the stakeholders. As much effort should be spent in measuring and tracking achievements as was spent on the initial design of the project and will be spent on the control and maintenance of the implementation.

BUY-IN/ADMINISTRATIVE SUPPORT

The first hurdle in initiating an EHR project involves acquiring administrative buy-in and support. The major challenge is engendering the realization that the true return on investment (ROI) of an EHR far exceeds the price tag of the hardware and software. The ROI comprises both cash (e.g., increasing productivity) and non-cash equivalents (e.g., decreased liability from decreased medical errors, improved patient care, better corporate image, and more free time for both clinicians and staff). Hence, it falls to the administrative leadership, in cooperation with a physician champion or practice manager, to appreciate all the benefits that readily justify the expenditures required for implementing an EHR.

Once a commitment has been made to purchase an EHR, the practice manager and/or physician leader is typically made accountable for all phases of the implementation: selection, installation, rollout, and optimization. This responsibility, however, may be delegated to the project leader. The leader needs to clearly understand the implications of the EHR, demonstrate commitment to keep the implementation within budget, attain human resource support and *sustain those allocations until all project milestones have been attained.* The leader should also communicate, clearly and often, the message that implementing an EHR is as much about a cultural shift as it is about connecting technologies and redesigning workflows.

In group practices, including a multi-specialty group practice, the clinician chosen as leader may become the project leader or EHR champion. This clinician should be respected by his or her colleagues, be able to dedicate sufficient time and energy to the project, and demonstrate commitment to finding a solution that satisfies the needs of the majority of the group. Sometimes, several key physicians from different practice areas should be tapped to serve collaboratively as leaders.

EHR CHAMPIONS

Not all physicians and staff will embrace EHR implementation. Therefore, it is important to have those who strongly support the EHR serve as champions to provide direction for the group, maintain ongoing day-to-day support, and encourage buy-in from the users. Perhaps the most crucial role for the EHR champion is to obtain buy-in from senior management who must support the project in order for it to succeed.

Champions must be identified early. Their roles in the EHR implementation must take precedence over their other office duties. Therefore, it may be necessary to temporarily relieve them of those other duties to give them enough time to encourage others in the office. In small practices the champion should be a physician or office manager who is respected by his or her colleagues and is able to dedicate sufficient time and energy to convincing the rest of the stakeholders.

It is *essential* that the champion remain actively engaged with other physicians and staff throughout the course of the implementation and even after the go-live date. Without such engagement and encouragement physicians and staff may resist implementation, fail to adapt to the EHR, and revert to old routines.

The champion need not be the *only* individual to promote change. He/she should be the office cheerleader and persuade others to become champions themselves.

A Case in Point

Montefiore Medical Center in the Bronx, NY, was one of the first hospitals to implement a systemwide computerized practitioner order entry (CPOE) system. The senior hospital administration found that measuring and reporting implementation achievements to all stakeholders was vital to the success of the EHR implementation. The medical center measured such EHR successes as appropriate inpatient utilization, prevention of adverse drug interactions and physician adherence to formularies. This helped create support from both the hospital leadership and the end-users of the EHR system and fostered a successful and aggressive implementation of the EHR system.

DIPLOMACY ABOVE ALL ELSE

When it comes to satisfying stakeholders, diplomacy is crucial. You may not be able to satisfy all stakeholders but you need to try. Reaching consensus in the majority may be the best that you can hope for. You cannot succeed without stakeholder support, whether it comes from the board of directors at a large hospital or from the nurse who takes your patients' blood pressures.

REACHING BUY-IN IS ONLY THE PRELUDE TO MAINTAINING IT

After obtaining initial stakeholder support, you must plan to maintain it. All stakeholders are affected by whether or not the EHR implementation is successful. In the office, for example, benefits such as error reduction and increased efficiency must be balanced against potential short and long-term costs. These costs include an initial reduction in workflow and additional time to train, and retrain staff. The shortfalls must be repeatedly communicated to everyone involved, soliciting agreement and continued commitment from all stakeholders.

MEASURING SUCCESS IS NOT JUST ABOUT "COST"

Besides balance sheet reporting, another way to measure success and to report it to the stakeholders is to use metrics *other* than revenue. Although often more obtuse than financial reporting, improvements in quality of care, reduction of medical errors, and the improvement in clinician and staff quality of life (the result of improved efficiency) are important measurements. The staff's satisfaction with the EHR system should also be measured and the implementation modified whenever necessary to increase that satisfaction.

CHAPTER 8

Phase 2: Analysis

UNDERSTANDING BUSINESS NEEDS

In the near future, government and other payors will require physicians to implement an EHR system into their practices. Although medical practice strategies will be forced to change as a result of this "cram down" process, it is far better to try to incorporate IT into the core of the business environment itself. If this occurs the implementation may stand a good chance at success.

Medical practices are driven by the need to become more efficient. Although part of a service industry, they place little emphasis on competing for business. They usually do not concern themselves with finding ways to achieve sustainable competitive advantage. Their patients, as customers, usually pay them with someone else's money, including employers, Medicare, Medicaid and commercial insurers. Most practices do not see business growth as a priority. They often reach a maximum steady state of patients and struggle to survive economically in the face of decreasing reimbursements. Instead of seeking growth, they seek a reduction in workload and achievement of a better lifestyle. Therefore, medical practices typically introduce technology to control and to manage operational activities. They seldom consider how technology fits into their business mission that, in most cases, is simply to take care of patients. Even to deliver care effectively, however, they may have to alter the structure and even the organization of the practice prior to the introduction of technology. The business structure must be reviewed, analyzed, and changed where necessary prior to EHR implementation. If this does not occur, then technology will be added to a dysfunctional business and merely create a technologically advanced, dysfunctional business.

Whether implementing the EHR for a single physician office or a 50-physician multi-specialty clinic, the resources necessary to attain the planned objective must first be defined and adequate sources identified before initiating the project.

ASSESSING THE PRACTICE

Analyzing the practice might reveal potential problems that can be corrected by the right EHR system. These include:

- Absence of adequate flowcharts or the ability to discern trends and patterns of disease
- Use of the antiquated SOAP (subjective, objective, assessment, plan) method approach; i.e., the need to migrate from an acute toward a preventive care approach
- Medical errors
- Medical omissions
- Lack of continuity of care
- Inefficient workflows
- Unnecessary variation in care
- Rising costs

These problems may be ameliorated by an effective EHR system, but these problems need to be addressed, and workflows changed, in order to make a smooth transition into electronic medical recordkeeping.

ANALYZING PROCESSES

Transitioning a small group or solo practice from paper to electronic records may require turning the practice upside down. No business economies will be achieved if the new system merely mimics the paper system. Every business process, both administrative and clinical, needs to be analyzed and understood. The practice should designate responsible individuals to evaluate their respective administrative or clinical workflows and how they might change in the electronic environment. Workflows may need to be changed to match the capabilities of the EHR.

One of the ways to identify how current processes and workflows will be affected by the EHR is to "follow the data." Review the paper health record and document how, by whom and at what stage the data are captured. By going through this analysis in the early stages of implementation, process gaps can be identified and workflows can be re-engineered before go-live. It is important to make sure that the current manual processes are efficient because automating inefficient manual processes may make them even more inefficient in an EHR environment.

IDENTIFYING RESOURCES

Resources, both monetary and human, are necessary to integrate the EHR into the existing system, control the scope of the project, allow for future expansion of data capacity, design the project and maintain a time schedule for implementation, provide adequate funding throughout the project, monitor the implementation for quality, hire and manage workers with required skills, communicate effectively with all stakeholders and assess the different kinds of risks that may occur throughout all phases of the implementation and establish the means to mitigate that risk.

A computerized practice is not mysteriously turned into a more efficient practice nor does it automatically provide better patient care. Information systems do not, by themselves, improve the practice. An EHR adds value only in conjunction with other factors, such as physician and staff participation and redesign of office workflow.

IDENTIFYING TECHNOLOGY

The technology assessment identifies discrepancies between the existing technical infrastructure (i.e., existing computer hardware and software) and the requirements of the proposed system. Key areas for assessment include:
- Existing hardware and infrastructure (e.g., wiring)
- System interfaces
- Point of contact devices (devices for inputting data)
- Clinician support services (technical assistance)

It may be more expensive to try to integrate a legacy system into the new technology than to operate both systems side by side during the transition phase. Electronic data interfaces (EDIs) may have to be developed and tested but will be less important as national standards are developed for interoperability between systems.

IDENTIFYING AND ANALYZING BARRIERS

Inadequate Budget

Allocating adequate resources represents the primary challenge facing medical practices attempting to implement an EHR.

Short-term Costs

The individual responsible for budgeting the cost of an EHR must remember to include the price of any wiring, electrical circuitry, phone or DSL service, ventilation, or other one-time costs. Exam and office space may not be large enough to accommodate PCs, printers, and peripherals, so a structural redesign/construction of the exam rooms, front office space, and lab space may be necessary. These are "sunk" costs and must be considered before purchasing a system.

Costs are also likely to be incurred when establishing or strengthening communications and acquiring new hardware and software to support the EHR. Existing computer equipment may need to be replaced. New technology, such as tablets and laptops, may need to be acquired to facilitate provider mobility.

Hidden costs are also relevant. These may be related to data conversion and training. There is also likely to be a short-term reduction in office productivity during the initial learning curve of the EHR system. Finally, a lack of in-house technical expertise may require the assistance of consultants for training.

Long-term Costs

Long-term costs must also be budgeted. These include the funds required to sustain the system after the first year. Equipment must be maintained, upgraded and/or replaced periodically. License fees will continue on an annual basis. Further technical assistance may be needed to address ongoing maintenance and upgrades. Finally, training new employees will be an ongoing expense unless a "super" user can be trained to train the rest of the staff.

Inadequate Skills and Experience

Most small medical practices do not have staff skilled in computer hardware and software. An outside consultant or vendor project manager may be necessary to ensure that all factors are considered early in the project. This individual will then facilitate oversight of all activities once the project is underway.

Most staff will have basic computer literacy skills such as using a keyboard and mouse, clicking/dragging, and navigating the computer's operating environment. They will require initial and maintenance training in an EHR system. The clinical staff who have been using a paper-based system may have difficulty learning the process changes associated with an EHR. Without careful and thorough communications between the person(s) with technical experience and the clinical staff there is a risk that poorly designed, inefficient paper processes will be converted to efficient, but still poorly designed, electronic processes.

There is a wide learning curve in implementing an EHR. The change from a legacy system, if one exists in the practice, to a new EHR will require that the staff master new skills. While it might appear necessary to develop instructional programs to learn those skills, outsourcing should be considered until they can be learned. Having such expertise in-house will minimize long-term dependence on consultants. Training can take the forms of live computer classes or online/CD resources supplemented by written documentation. If skills are outsourced, the project must plan for assimilation of those skills after a reasonable period of time. Time will vary according to the experience and trainability of the staff, but the transition from outsourcing to in-sourcing should not take longer than six months.

CHAPTER 9

Phase 3: Design

Betty Crocker does not make a soufflé. There are no out-of-the-box solutions to managing a clinical practice. It takes planning, human involvement, and a great deal of patience.

GETTING STARTED: ASSESSING THE PRACTICE'S READINESS TO GO ELECTRONIC

The definition of a paperless practice is not uniform throughout the healthcare industry, so a detailed definition of expectations is mandatory. Being paperless will require incorporating the existing paper records into the EHR; the practice must accept that it will take time to populate each patient's EHR. In addition, being paperless may require integrating any existing practice management system (e.g., billing, scheduling) with the EHR and potentially interfacing with ancillary systems (e.g., laboratory, radiology, pharmacy, etc.).

At the beginning stages of an EHR initiative, it is essential to analyze how the clinical and office staff accomplish their respective tasks. The next step is to determine what needs to remain the same and what needs to change to improve workflow and the efficiency of the organization. Such analysis must be an integral part of the EHR strategy and implementation; otherwise, the organization will not achieve its goals for creating a more effective and profitable environment.

It is also important to define how success with the EHR will be measured. Taking the time to define success at the beginning of the process will prevent issues related to unmet expectations.

WORKFLOW ANALYSIS

In many healthcare organizations, transitioning from paper-based patient care to an EHR represents embracing an entirely novel clinical workflow. It is essential that the new workflows implement both current best care practice and the practice's strategic objectives. The assessment team should evaluate the practice's workflow prior to implementation, and then identify the discrepancies between current and best practice, or ideal, workflow.

For example, the analysis might evaluate workflow according to how physicians and nurses obtain data and produce documentation, how physicians order medications, or the path the patient follows through the office during a visit. Such an analysis should identify what changes should be made to such "clinical processes," and consequently recognize challenges that will result from such organizational change. Key points to address when analyzing workflow include:

- *Departure and omissions from current workflow:* Document current workflow, and identify which workflow processes will be impacted by the proposed EHR, as well as how these processes will be impacted. Ensure no clinically necessary steps are omitted.
- *Care quality:* Develop mechanisms to enforce and measure compliance with evidence based medical guidelines that reinforce clinical best practices.
- *Care standardization:* Identify workflow processes to be standardized across the practice, such as clinical forms. This is especially true for multidiscipline group practices.
- *Clinical decision support:* Define the tools to assist clinicians in reaching medical decisions; identify how the proposed EHR implements these.

Several studies have shown that physician and overall office/clinic productivity will decrease during the early phases of the implementation. This temporary decrease in efficiency must be considered when designing the implementation plan and communicated to all physicians and ancillary personnel so that they do not become discouraged or frustrated. Temporary increases in expenses and decreases in budgeted revenue should be anticipated.

Physicians' schedules should be lightened to accommodate the decrease in efficiency during the ramp up period. Physicians who are compensated based on productivity can be severely affected financially during the implementation, so compensation systems must be modified to accommodate this transitional period.

PROJECT PLANNING

Be Prepared

A well-designed project plan is imperative to the success of the EHR implementation. Once developed, the project plan should be saved as a baseline. The project manager (and indeed, all participants) must become comfortable with modifying the plan as new information becomes available. Be prepared, in fact, for an iterative project planning process as the team becomes more educated. It is also helpful to break the large, complex project into smaller, more manageable "chunks" or subprojects. The pilot project is one of those "chunks." Tasks should be defined in sufficient detail to enable adequate project control. All participants should reach consensus on the contents and sign off on the work plan.

The concept of a project plan may be new to some members of the implementation team, so it is important to assess how well they follow to the plan and complete assigned tasks. If small tasks are neglected or milestones not reached it is likely that larger, more significant assignments are problematic. Team members may object more strenuously to the overall project management structure than to the actual tasks assigned to them. Therefore, it is important to focus on those tasks by assigning them early in the project and asking for feedback. The roles associated with those tasks should be clear and unambiguous. They should have a clearly discernible purpose and contribute significantly to the goals of the EHR implementation. Problems that arise should be addressed immediately.

Project managers need to intercede early if someone misses a delivery date for a small assignment. Face-to-face discussions with the individual, in a constructive and encouraging tone, will help compel him/her to deliver on a more difficult and significant task later in the project. Friendly, cooperative communication at the beginning of an EHR project will help anticipate and avoid the risk of failure.

Early task assignment will help identify everyone's capabilities. There may be team members who have never worked with the project leader so the project leader should spend as much one-on-one time as possible with team members. He/she should constantly assess their skills and performance. It is often helpful to assign new team members to work with more seasoned staff so that culture, skills, and core competencies can be readily learned.

The Planning Process

The planning process should begin by developing a comprehensive, extensive plan of actions and milestones. It is beneficial to detail the steps required to move to a fully electronic system. The plan should be reviewed regularly and should be flexible enough to be modified for any new processes and/or workflows that may become necessary. This plan should clearly designate the resources (individuals or entities) that will be responsible for each phase and task of the implementation.

Definitive dates for completion of each phase of the project should be set only after the detailed plan is developed and resources are identified. The go-live date may begin after all patient demographics have been entered into the EHR.

It is beneficial to take the time to visualize how each task in the practice workflow will be accomplished in the new paperless environment. The more time spent during planning, the more likely all clinical and non-clinical staff will understand the extensiveness of the impending change. The project manager and all senior management should encourage the staff to think creatively and allow them to offer suggestions for a smooth implementation. The implementation plan should be reviewed at all staff meetings and modified, if necessary, if it can be improved. Staff who will be using the system may be able to warn of pitfalls resulting from the implementation design. Potential scenarios should be developed at these meetings to ensure that unforeseen problems are more likely to be anticipated and avoided.

Five Planning Pitfalls to Avoid
Pitfall 1: Unsatisfactory Project Management and Control
Identify individuals in both formal and informal leadership positions

who are capable of facilitating or blocking the implementation. The facilitators should be encouraged to become EHR champions. Those who might impede the implementation should become part of a behavioral change program to achieve their buy-in. If buy-in cannot be achieved by the time implementation begins, resistant staff may have to be replaced.

Pitfall 2: Lack of Communication

Every practice has an internal culture that dictates how communication occurs. The culture includes both clinical and ancillary staff and will affect their tolerance of change, sense of teamwork, attitudes toward technology and the leadership style of managers.

Pitfall 3: Incomplete Goal Identification

If the expectations for the EHR are not clearly delineated, role confusion may develop and impede the implementation.

Pitfall 4: Underestimating Project Complexity

Underestimating how complex a project will be to implement can result in increased costs, extended time to go-live, and staff disillusionment.

Pitfall 5: Failure to Re-engineer Workflow

If the workflow is not improved prior to EHR implementation, do not expect the technology to improve it. Dysfunctional workflows are not miraculously corrected; they get worse, further complicating the implementation.

Planning Requirements

EHR implementations require skill, talent, and experience in a few critical areas. The implementation must be thoroughly planned and workflow clearly understood. Re-engineering of workflow and/or the EHR system may be required at times. An enabling relationship must be developed between management and staff. Goals should be effectively communicated and a mutual interest in learning should be engendered.[17]

In addition, strategic business objectives should be defined and shared with staff. Milestones for completing each phase of the project should be communicated and consensus obtained from all involved.

Milestones should be set realistically; most IT system implementations never progress as quickly as originally planned. It is also important to recognize that most new users usually progress along the learning curve more slowly than expected. Accordingly, the practice should understand the potential impact to its patient load. If these processes are successfully initiated, everyone will develop a realistic attitude towards the EHR and the positive changes it will bring to the practice.

CHAPTER 10

Phase 4: Managing Change

PROCESS CHANGES

EHR implementation is likely to require major changes in the practice. Workflows will change, paper-processing activities will change, and entirely new routines and activities will be born. Anticipate that there will be challenges in reaching consensus regarding some of the processes. For example, providers will disagree on the setup of appointment panels and the templates designed for history and progress notes. The EHR system should be flexible enough to be able to make changes that will satisfy the majority of users in the practice.

An especially challenging workflow change for the clinician is entering EHR data at the time of the visit and not later, which is typically the case with paper charts. With paper charts, clinicians often make notations later in the day or after hours. This process defeats the advantages of having an integrated, automated billing module. The redesign and change in such a process can cause frustration but good communications between the clinical and technical staff may help temper resistance. Encouraging on-going evaluations and providing feedback with permission to make improvements will further reduce resistance.

Even before the implementation begins it is critical that both technical and workflow processes are evaluated. It is essential to understand how any redesign from an EHR will impact the flow of activities in the office. For instance, if a legacy billing system is to be maintained, the workflow involved in moving between two systems must be carefully mapped out. If new workflows need to be designed the practice should do so as early as possible so that the new processes are incorporated into user training.

PUSH (PLANNED CHANGE) VERSUS PULL (EMERGENT CHANGE)

Any major project such as the implementation of an EHR must be developed based on knowledge gained from previous attempts to implement change within the organization. Change is a reaction—a sequence of events triggered by a need. The change may be planned, in which case someone with authority *pushes* it through the organization, or it may be unplanned, where an emergent need *pulls* on forces to make the change happen.

Whether change is pushed or pulled is often determined by an organization's culture. Planned change is intentional—a formal, top-down approach, based on the identification of a problem and implementing a solution. Planned change often comes from within the organization. It is a proactive and deliberate process in response to a new opportunity, a shift in business goals, external pressures, and/or environmental change. Planned change requires strong leadership and effective communication with all staff. If not communicated and coordinated correctly, the planned change may be interpreted by the staff as unanticipated change. In other words, without "buy-in" from those who will be affected by the change, the process may be written off as "whim."

Unplanned change can be divided into two major categories; unanticipated and emergent. Unanticipated change is unplanned and unforeseen. It may derive from a previously unrecognized need within the organization or it may be the result of macro forces working from outside the organization. For example, HIPAA "pulled" change through healthcare organizations simply by changing the law. Healthcare providers had no choice but to modify the way they do business.

Emergent change is a proactive response to unforeseen circumstances and "emerges" from the needs of the end-users. Emergent change does not automatically imply it is unmanaged; instead it is based on the idea that change is inevitable. Systems and processes are designed from the "bottom-up" to respond to change as it occurs. Aarts, Doorewaard, and Berg suggest that the final outcome of the EHR implementation process is unpredictable because of organizational dynamics and complexity. They note that the "process of change never stops. Even when the implementation is formally finished, users will still shape and craft the information system to fit their particular requirements or interests. This often occurs in a way that was unanticipated even by the designers." [18]

The ability of an organization to respond to the constant process of change starts with a vision. This vision must anticipate change and nurture an organizational culture that accepts change as inevitable and hopefully even desirable. As a result, the proactive organization puts processes in place to respond to change. Medical offices must develop this culture in order to deal with anticipated changes in the healthcare industry. They will most certainly need to do this if they are to successfully implement EHRs in their offices. This culture must promote a proactive and positive attitude toward change. The office must become flexible and adapt quickly to change. It must be able to identify new strategies and incorporate lessons learned from past experiences.

The constant potential and need for change is characteristic of the modern healthcare environment that is continually being pushed or pulled through the change process. Any organizational culture that supports and encourages adaptation and change in response to environmental pressures will be best suited to compete and survive in this environment. The medical organizations that can do this will become the successful early adopters of EHRs. The rest will simply have to wait for the federal "Big Stick" and the change, without a proactive approach, will not be easy or pleasant.

MANAGING CHANGE

Change will occur only when an organization is able to define the benefits it will derive from the change. The user must discern visible benefits either in terms of improved workflow efficiencies or a perception that the change will improve patient care, or both. Therefore, when planning an EHR, the specific needs of each user (e.g., clinicians and clinical support staff), must be addressed. Physicians in particular are integral to the process of enabling change. Therefore, they must perceive a value not only to the practice but to the delivery of quality patient care. Physicians must be involved from the beginning, before decisions are finalized. *Most importantly, a practice should refrain from giving in to the innate desire to force the new system to mimic the current system.*

Change management involves people, processes, and technology and extends well beyond just the system and information technology. A plan to manage change should do the following:

1. Define the required or desired change.
2. Identify, define, and quantify results expected from change.
3. Specify the reason for change.
4. Describe what the practice will look like after the changes are complete.
5. Ensure that the change supports strategic business objectives and initiatives.
6. Identify the leadership to promote and manage the change and provide for accommodation and training.
7. Identify the desired time frame and responsible parties for implementing change.
8. Ensure the delivery of adequate resources.
9. Change behavior and culture when appropriate.

CHANGE MANAGEMENT FOR IMPLEMENTATION

It cannot be stressed enough that human factors weigh heavily in the success or failure of an EHR implementation. Management of people and change factors may be more important than technology decisions. Therefore, when implementing an EHR it is important to consider the four "change factors" suggested by Chin:[19]

1. Organizational decisionmaking and support;
2. Project management;
3. Communications; and
4. Training.

Organizational Decisionmaking and Support

The front-line staff should be empowered to make high level decisions regarding the EHR implementation. This includes the design and content of the EHR since their knowledge of how the EHR will link to their work will affect the success of the project. Often, however, workflows are not efficient and must be re-engineered prior to EHR implementation.

Organizational policies should also reinforce the desired outcomes of the EHR. As an example, the system should notify clinicians of the formulary status of prescribed medications so that non-formulary medications are either not prescribed or referred to prior authorization.

Project Management

The staff may view the EHR as an electronic aid capable of performing more than what it is designed to do. This unrealistic view is known as "scope creep." Lorenzi and Riley suggest that scope creep is derived from a lack of clarity in overall system objectives and can lead to confusion, re-work and delay.[20] Systems and project managers should consider how to translate business objectives into system objectives and then carefully phase them into the implementation. The EHR project team can avoid missing critical steps by thinking through the practice's workflow from patient sign-in to the completion of the clinical visit.

Communications

The success of the EHR implementation will depend on good communication and feedback. Obtaining feedback from stakeholders before, during, and after implementation is critical. This helps to continue buy-in and motivation from everyone involved with the project. Feedback from surveys of clinicians using the system may lead to opportunities for improvement.

According to Chin, "bridgers" are a group of stakeholders who know how to bridge the cultural gap between the end-user, the organization, and the new information technology.[19] Bridgers excel at identifying the tradeoffs between functionality, effort and risk. Thus, they are an important part of the communications feedback loop to maintain buy-in from system users.

Training

Most clinicians forget much of what they learned soon after EHR training, retaining only enough to get by. Chin suggests that more than 50% of clinicians remember less than 50% of what they were taught during the initial training.[19] Therefore, training must be ongoing and repetitive. The EHR system, the practice workflows, and advances in medical treatment are always changing. Thus, it is important for the office to provide updates in the training of both clinicians and staff.

OVERCOMING RESISTANCE: ORGANIZATIONAL

Communications and Champions

Resistance to changing the status quo is largely driven by fear, uncertainty, and doubt. Training, communication, and information can help to reduce these factors. Nothing removes doubt more quickly than clear, concise, and repetitive communication. Weekly e-mails outlining progress, offering tips, alerting selected groups of impending change, and explaining the values of new features are one effective means of communication. A positive story cannot be told often enough. If e-mail is not yet available, a bulletin board with daily or weekly progress notes can be used.

The transformation of an organization begins with the transformation of individuals. Implementation teams can facilitate individual transformation by helping users learn what technological change will mean to them in their own work processes. Roles should be clearly outlined and communicated so that there is no ambiguity.

Members of the implementation team are usually champions for change; they fully embrace it and are able to influence others to do the same. Change champions should be cultivated and nurtured. They will provide ongoing communications and progress at the grass roots level.

Speed Kills

A practice should implement the EHR only as rapidly as the staff can learn the new system and tolerate the changes it brings. Progress must be steady and not fragmented. Stopping training and re-tracing steps may prolong the agony of using a dual paper and electronic system.

The practice must also be willing to accept that there will be a loss of productivity during training as clinicians and staff become comfortable with using the system. Patient loads may need to be reduced or staffing increased during this time.

Physician Incentives

Physicians are motivated by patient care but are paid for results. If the practice compensation model is such that an individual's revenue stream may be adversely affected by a fall in productivity, the implementation plan must at least maintain the physician's current compensation.

OVERCOMING RESISTANCE: INDIVIDUAL

Energy should be focused on establishing the value of adopting an EHR, not only for the practice but for individual staff members as well. Facts, training, and education are the greatest weapons for combating resistance. Do not allow personal issues to enter discussions; they should be focused on reasons for the decisions, known facts and desired outcomes.

Typical resistance to an EHR can be derived from the following:

- *Lack of clinician acceptance:* Lack of acceptance is usually related to fear of the unknown. This can be reduced through training and education.
- *Concerns about inability to align workflow with the EHR:* Workflow should be reviewed during the analysis phase. Its migration into the EHR system should be carefully planned and implemented in steps.
- *Concerns that automation of clinical charting requires more time than paper charting:* Even if recording data requires more time during the patient visit, retrieving information is simplified and faster. Many EHRs today are designed so that documentation takes no more time during the visit than paper charting. In addition, electronic charts are not misplaced and important information is presented in a format that allows clinical decisions to be reached more readily.
- *Lack of uniform standards or incomplete documentation of clinical services:* A well-structured EHR will render more complete and uniform documentation than current paper systems.

DEALING WITH RESISTANCE

Senior management should not disregard the natural progression that employees go through when major change occurs in the workplace. These changes can mimic the five stages of grieving suggested by Elisabeth Kubler-Ross: denial, anger, bargaining, depression, and acceptance.[21] Practices that use coercion or punishment to change behavior offer little to assist employees through these stages. As a result, employees are stopped at the bargaining stage and resistance will continue by reverting to, and maintaining, anger. Though overt resistance may disappear, clandestine attempts to disrupt the changes in the organization become rampant and spread rapidly through the organization's grapevine.

Two methods to overcome active and passive resistance are to enhance communication and promote participation in the problem-solving process. By doing so, employee buy-in is more likely to occur.

One framework that has been proposed is to engage the resistant employee(s) in an alliance that leads to an acceptable solution.[22]

The first step in the process of overcoming resistance is for the project leader to be prepared. He/she must know what the project needs in order to be successful. Next, the leader must communicate, clearly and concisely, the purpose and goals for the EHR implementation.

Employee concerns must be explored and acknowledged. This will give legitimacy to those concerns and keep employees focused on the implementation. Their issues must be mirrored back to them so that they know the project leader understands their concerns.

Next, the project leader must determine how to respond to employee concerns; they will expect action. The project leader must communicate the actions that will be taken to resolve the problems.

Finally, the project leader must obtain closure. Commitment to action is not enough; he/she must follow through, resolve the employee issues, then follow up to ensure that their needs have been met.

CHAPTER 11

The Project Manager

The decisions to identify, hire, or outsource an individual as the project manager should occur as soon as the decision has been made to implement an EHR. The project manager will immediately become responsible for the design phase and the following nine aspects of the implementation:

1. Integration of project
2. Scope of project
3. Time of project
4. Cost of project
5. Quality of project
6. Human resources needs
7. Communication needs
8. Procurement needs
9. Risk assessment

INTEGRATION

Bringing the EHR into the organization will require the concerted effort of many individuals. The champion is typically the office manager or senior physician/partner. The project manager may be either or may be selected from someone else on staff. The project manager may also work for the vendor and be appointed by mutual consent of the practice and the vendor. The successful planning of the EHR project, however, requires the input of *all* participants.

SCOPE

The project's scope must first be defined in order to anticipate the present and future resources needed for implementation. The practice must decide what aspects of clinical care will be included in the EHR and how the EHR will integrate with the practice's business mission. This defines the scope of the project.

TIMING

The project schedule should allow enough time for adequate training of *all* users including part time employees and those with staggered work schedules. The time allotted must be uninterrupted. This may require hiring temporary employees to substitute for ancillary staff during the early stages of implementation.

COST

Too often the budget for the project is insufficient and results in a failed EHR implementation. This not only squanders capital but also loses the support of the stakeholders, including staff.

An under-funded budget is sometimes the result of errors in estimating the fixed and variable costs of hardware and software. It may also be the result of underestimating the true return on investment (ROI) from implementing an EHR. Therefore the EHR champion or senior management must calculate the true ROI, including both cash and non-cash equivalents.

Cash is derived from increased productivity including an increased flow of patients, more accurate coding and billing, and more effective collection of charges. Non-cash equivalents bring indirect revenue to the practice. Such equivalents include decreased liability from fewer medical errors, improved quality of care, more personal time for clinicians and staff, more usable physical space due to elimination of paper records, and a better image for the practice.

When considering costs, software, hardware, and human resources must be addressed. Human resource costs are spent on instructors and temporary staff to stand in while permanent staff is being trained.

Indirect costs arise from decreased productivity during the early stages of EHR implementation.

Software costs have a fixed price and can easily be estimated. In contrast, hardware costs may be more difficult to estimate because of future changes in storage requirements.

When budgeting the design and implementation phases of EHR implementation, the practice must understand the users' needs and workflow. In addition, the project manager must consider the expected growth in the practice as a result of using the EHR.

QUALITY

An EHR can be divided into three parts:
1. Data collection
2. Data retrieval
3. Data presentation

Inadequate methods for collecting data will hamper efforts to retrieve them later and/or lead to incomplete data gaps. The most important aspect of quality, however, is how well the data is presented to the users: Graphical User Interface (GUI) technology can present data in ways that decrease errors and minimizes physician liability as patient care ultimately improves.

HUMAN RESOURCES

An EHR implementation will need commitment from many dedicated individuals. Few medical practices, however, have enough staff capable of installing an EHR and providing the initial training. They must often rely on outside consultants but the additional expense can be significant.

Employees soon become aware that they are now fulfilling two job requirements: one for their daily role and one for learning a new system. Dedicated assignment of adequate employee resources to all phases of the project (designing, training, initiating, building, testing, and maintaining) is mandatory for a successful EHR implementation.

COMMUNICATION

Lack of communication and failure to communicate effectively are among the most often-cited reasons for project failure. Constant and effective communication between the project leader and end-users is essential throughout all phases of the EHR implementation. The leader must not only communicate but must also *listen* to every concern and idea from any potential end-user; the best solution to a problem may come from anyone at any level in the organization. Project leaders must demonstrate permissive leadership qualities and create an environment in which ideas can percolate up to the top of the organization instead of from the top down.

The project charter is an excellent communication tool. It should detail the "who, what, when, where, how, and why" of the EHR implementation and should be modified and expanded as the need arises. The charter informs the stakeholders of the goals expected from the implementation, who is participating in the project, the roles and hierarchy in the project, the steps necessary to reach each milestone, when the project will be completed, the go-live date, and where and when changes will occur in workflow.

PROCUREMENT

The project leader must understand and meet the software and hardware demands of the EHR system. Pre-tested hardware (e.g., workstations and scanners selected in the design phase) needs to be provided on schedule. Equipment that has not been tested should not be used; any unexpected hardware problems may lead to confusion and loss of confidence in the EHR implementation. The hardware selected must be appropriate in quantity and functionality. Full redundancy and backup is mandatory. Ease of input and retrieval of data and expandable storage capacity is essential. The critical aspects of EHR technology will be discussed in Chapter 12.

RISK ASSESSMENT

The project manager must identify and anticipate the risks from EHR implementation. He/she must plan for effective means of addressing any problems that might arise. Systems and processes to handle emergencies and disasters must be established and, if possible, tested prior to the go-live date.

Scope of the Organization

Vendors and consultants brought into the planning process must have a detailed understanding of the settings, staffing, structure and workflows·required by the practice. Strategies for communicating and managing upcoming changes are as critical for the small practice as they are for large enterprises. Everyone who will be impacted by these changes must develop an understanding of how the EHR will alter their workflows, impact their jobs, and improve the quality of care they deliver to their patients.

CHAPTER 12

Phase 5: Selection and Procurement

There is no one "best" combination of hardware, software, and processing model to address all of the practice's needs. Each practice, therefore, must consider the individual components required to best operate its business and provide care for its patients. The pros and cons of each EHR system should be analyzed based upon the individual practice's size, number of sites, budget constraints, risk tolerance, and other unique factors.

Customization of the EHR system is to be expected but should be done early so that future customization is infrequent. The design of the EHR should be flexible enough to accommodate variations in workflows. Consistent, accurate, and reliable data must be maintained at the highest level to ensure data integrity and the highest quality of patient care.

When selecting the right hardware and software for the medical practice's needs, it is important to analyze exactly what those needs are. The practice must do the following:

1. Appreciate the scope of solutions and their capabilities;
2. Know the long-term cost;
3. Understand the advantages and disadvantages of various solutions; and

4. Be able to verify and determine whether vendor products meet the practice's needs.

In addition, the practice should develop a plan to carry out the following:

1. Obtain quotations from vendors;
2. Evaluate vendor solutions in a way that ensures that vendors present their systems in "apples-to-apples" terms;
3. Score the results of demos in a meaningful way;
4. Consider how to minimize risk in selecting an EHR;
5. Consider how to evaluate the vendor's performance according to the contract; and
6. Consider how to minimize the risk should a vendor go out of business.

TECHNOLOGY

Early efforts to implement information technology in healthcare were driven by the need to *automate* existing processes such as typing and "number crunching." However, once we recognized the fact that healthcare organizations produce and consume massive amounts of data, IT was redirected to managing *information*.

Today, IT experts recognize that healthcare, as a business, is more complex than anyone realized. In order to address this complexity, business transformation and business improvement must be consistent with the business *strategy*. We now define this strategy as *knowledge management* and seek ways to automate it. For the small medical practice, the solution is the EHR.

EHRs have been described over the past few decades; some vendors and physicians made early attempts to integrate them into the practice of medicine. However, only during the past few years have improvements in EHR technology made integration feasible. The goal of having real-time, clinically relevant information delivered in a manner consistent with the daily life of a busy clinician is now a reality.

Some of the key technological trends that have enabled this transformation include:

- Hardware:
  - Increased power and expanded functionality of personal computers;
  - Continued reduction in hardware cost;
  - The emergence of smaller, more flexible portable devices for data entry and viewing such as PDAs and tablets;
  - The emergence of low-cost, increased bandwidth, wireless technology that enables clinicians to move between multiple sites; and
  - Increased capabilities of patient home-monitoring devices and ability to remotely collect the information necessary for rendering clinical decisions.
- Software:
  - The development of tools and standards to help ensure information security and patient confidentiality;
  - The attempt to develop standards for collecting and sharing clinical data; and
  - The initiation of regulatory requirements to maintain audit trails and track access.

These trends have only begun to create the "perfect storm" of technological capabilities that will support the unique needs of an EHR system in the U.S. today. It is up to the federal government in collaboration with the private sector to create and enforce these standards so that all EHR systems will be interoperable.

INFRASTRUCTURE AND INTEROPERABILITY

As noted, there is no single "best" medical IT solution or combination of hardware, processing model, and software; each solution has advantages and disadvantages. A practice must first define what it expects from an EHR and, more importantly, what it *requires* from an EHR. In order to best operate its business and provide care for its patients, a medical office must establish an information technology infrastructure based on its in-house capabilities and needs. It is important, therefore, to identify the needs of each clinician for hardware (e.g., tablet PC, notebook PC, desktop PC) and software interfaces (GUIs). This will ensure that information is readily available and efficiently delivered through the correct system.

The pros and cons of each contemplated solution should be developed based upon the practice's size, number of sites, budget constraints (both upfront and ongoing costs), tolerance for risk, technical staff support, space requirements, "locality" of information, and other unique factors.

Typical processing models include self-contained systems (run on a local computer or group of computers physically linked); application service provider (run by a vendor, typically at a remote facility); intranet, (local or internal network); and Internet (World Wide Network).

System software can be proprietary (belonging to a specific vendor) or open source (no individual owner). Most healthcare software vendors today use propriety software, although open source software is gaining momentum in some areas. Proprietary software is not to be feared when considering change. It is the portability of the data and information that is critical to a practice rather than the underlying software used.

Regardless of which software is chosen, the software must address both security and data interchange standards (e.g., HIPAA, HL7). Software that does not comply with security standards is a liability to the practice and software that cannot "write" to a data interchange standard will not be able to transfer data to and from laboratories, pharmacies, health plans, other healthcare providers, billing entities and public health departments.

An EHR should be able to interface with other systems, including legacy databases. You should be aware, however, that interfacing between different vendor systems is difficult, and developing standards and testing interfaces are an important part of implementation. EHR vendor certification will require that systems are capable of interoperability if they are to pass certification testing.

To be interoperable, an EHR will need to send and receive information from such internal and external systems as:
1. Patient administration systems;
2. Point-of-care clinical systems;
3. Ambulatory information systems; and
4. Community based health information systems.

The practice should understand what is necessary for communication between these entities:

1. A unique patient identifier (NHIN);
2. Standards for nomenclature (e.g., SNOMED, LOINC);
3. Standards for interface (e.g., HL7);
4. Current and proposed communications infrastructure; and
5. Provider technologies.

The current standards are supported by organizations such as the Healthcare Information and Management Systems Society (HIMSS), Certification Commission for Health Information Technology (CCHIT), governmental agencies and others, while additional standards are being developed.

EHR systems must, at a minimum, incorporate the current standards and be poised to adopt new standards as they are developed. Be certain that interconnectivity exists between the EHR system, current systems, and data repositories. An EHR must be able to record and report data including patient demographics and clinical information, laboratory and x-ray results, and financial information. Once all reporting standards are adopted, the EHR must be able to interface with other systems and communicate that data.

INTERFACE DEVELOPMENT

If the practice already has a legacy system, the challenges of interfacing that system to a new EHR are diverse. Numerous unique interfaces may be required to connect the EHR with external systems. Older systems may not contain the latest HL7 (Health Level Seven) standards and, if they do, they may possess different interpretations or applications of those standards. The business logic of different systems may not process data in the same way. Therefore, it is necessary to ensure that the workflow from the system sending data matches that of the system receiving data. In most cases, the cost of interfacing with legacy systems will be substantial.

If integration between the EHR and a disparate system cannot be accomplished or the legacy system needs to be maintained alongside the new system, the practice must be sensitive to the frustration the users may experience. A Clinical Context Object Workgroup (CCOW) may assist in dealing with multiple systems.

The CCOW Standard is an element of HL7 that is vendor independent. It allows clinical applications to share information at the point of care. Using a technique called context management, CCOW provides a unified view of the patient information stored in disparate electronic systems. When these systems are connected in a CCOW environment, the clinician can sign onto one system and be simultaneously signed on to all others in the CCOW group. The clinician then sees a combined view of the patient on a single screen.

Remember that technology is just a tool, not the solution. However, the choices made with regard to the technology will impact the quality of care, productivity, and profitability of the practice.

SECURITY AND ACCESS

Addressing security issues must be part of the EHR design prior to actual implementation. Security should extend from local devices to remote access (e.g., access from home and other locations). Information must be kept confidential at all times. Security of access and privacy of information is not only good practice but is made mandatory by government regulations and law.

The degree to which patients have access to the EHR system must also be considered prior to implementation. Practice decisions regarding patient access to information should also be part of a risk analysis. Although patient access is important, it is best avoided at initial roll out of the system. It is prudent to take the time to fine-tune a new EHR system before subjecting it to external scrutiny.

GRAPHICAL USER INTERFACES

Human interfaces (e.g., graphical user interfaces) require special consideration with respect to their design, development, implementation, and testing within the EHR implementation process. Not only are these interfaces critical, they also help to determine the quality of patient care; every channel for data must be thoroughly tested before relying on it for clinical decisions.

All system interfaces should be installed and tested in a manner consistent with the overall implementation schedule. The EHR vendor and the practice will coordinate such installations under the auspices of the project leader in order to minimize disruptions.

Interfaces are usually required for a large assortment of functions in medical practices from financial accounting to ordering laboratory tests. A phased approach should be used to prioritize then schedule the connectivity and integration requirements. Every aspect of creating the interfaces, from early planning and strategy, through development and scripting, to final acceptance, should be part of the overall project plan.

REPORTING (DATA "MINING")

Reporting can only be accomplished if data are captured and discretely organized in a standardized manner. A health data "dictionary" should be created in preparation for EHR implementation. Once the process of adding health data to the dictionary is completed, authorized users should be assigned to update the information and to notify other users of the changes.

CLINICAL CONTENT

It is important to ensure that the data contained in an EHR system is presented in a manner that enhances the quality of patient care. Data entry needs to be accurate, fast, and efficient. Standardized medical vocabularies can enhance the accuracy and efficiency of data entry and simplify the exchange of information.

Questions that should be asked of the vendor include:

- Does the EHR software require the practice to create/build the clinical content?
- Is it standardized?
- Can the user customize?
- How is the clinical data available for reporting?
- Is the data specialty-specific?
- Is there a way to track revisions/additions to content?
- How is clinical data entered (macros, templates, drop-down boxes, radial buttons, etc.)?

CUSTOMIZATION

To adequately and appropriately design an EHR, it is necessary to first obtain information about the practice's existing systems and procedures. This may be accomplished through on-site inspections, interviews, and meetings with appropriate personnel. Information the practice should have available at the outset includes computer network diagrams, architectural building drawings, hardware and software systems in use, protocols and clinical practice procedures, business systems, employee resources, and future requirements.

The software should provide options for customizing screens and for documenting and presenting clinical information. In addition, the vendor should outline a process for incorporating future design changes that are beyond the scope of the current version of the software.

Finally, the design of the EHR should be able to accommodate workflow and procedures that may vary from one office to another. If so, customization should be done early in the implementation.

PAPER VERSUS DIGITAL TECHNOLOGY

It may be necessary to continue to document patient records on paper until the EHR system is implemented and running effectively. The practice must decide whether it wants to eliminate paper completely or retain some elements of paper documentation.

Information flows more smoothly through an EHR system. However, some delivery of care may occur outside of an integrated system and paper documentation will still be part of the process.

DATA CONVERSION

Practices should develop internal policies for determining how paper records will be integrated into the EHR system. One way is to scan records, convert them to PDF formats, and attach them directly to the patient's electronic record. Another is to isolate the data from the written documentation and enter it by hand into the electronic patient record. The latter procedure, though laborious, will enable the data to become a functional part of the patient's record. All database conversions are unique, and technical staff from the software vendor should provide assistance.

MAINTENANCE AGREEMENTS

A full service contract for both hardware and software is essential to continued success of the EHR implementation. Consideration should be given to how often the office is open and whether or not the clinicians must access the system after hours. Often, a 24 hour, 7 days per week contract for emergency repair should already be in place when implementation begins. The vendor should have 24/7 telephone triage availability to respond to the system users.

Hardware and software maintenance contracts may be separate. The hardware may be serviced by the vendor, the hardware manufacturer, or a third party vendor. Software maintenance is normally performed by the EHR vendor but may be transferred by the vendor to a third party.

The cost varies by the choice of response time, availability, and site of service. Round-the-clock availability and same day on-site service will be the most costly and may not be necessary in most small practices open only eight hours, five days a week. A choice of service contracts will be available and should be discussed with the EHR vendors before implementation begins.

PLANNING FOR THE "WORST"

What happens if a vendor goes out of business? Who will maintain the system? Who will upgrade it?

These questions will soon become moot if the practice purchases a "certified" EHR system. The Certifying Commission for Health Information Technology (CCHIT), formed in 2004 and authorized by the federal government in October 2005, has the responsibility for certifying EHR systems based on accepted functionality, interoperability, security, and reliability. Any certified EHR system must be interoperable with other systems. Therefore, a practice may be able to substitute one system for another without having to change hardware systems. In addition, newer technology has allowed EHR systems to be web browser-based and completely portable.

Although the risk of a vendor going out of business is less today than previously, it is still prudent to include a clause in the vendor contract that provides for specific performance, penalties, and remuneration if the vendor goes out of business or a shift in responsibility to the new company if it is sold.

CHAPTER 13

Phase 6: Installation and Set-Up

You can't bake a great soufflé until you have all the ingredients, and you can't have all the ingredients until you can afford to buy them. Once you get them home you can't prepare them without the right utensils; you can't bake them without an oven; you can't turn the oven on without electricity. And, if you think that's enough to bake a great soufflé, you're wrong. You need a recipe prepared by experts to help you turn a failed attempt into a glorious repast.

EHR implementation is the great soufflé of healthcare. It will take time, preparation, patience, money, dedication and skill and, above all, a great recipe for making it all work.

GUIDING PRINCIPLE FOR STARTING THE IMPLEMENTATION PROCESS: MORE THAN MEETS THE EYE

Information systems are *not technical systems*. They are *human* activity systems.

Because implementations involve people, expecting perfection during an implementation is unrealistic and will undermine success. Being flexible and adapting to change is crucial. Do not allow exaggerated attention to details to jeopardize the overall implementation goal: keep it simple and strive for excellence, not perfection. Seek

73

advice, but do not let desire to reach perfect consensus slow progress; sometimes decisions must be made by one person.

Physician practices must be prepared to change established business processes, not merely automate them. If the office is dysfunctional without adding the complexity of technology, just think how dysfunctional it will be with technology. Technology will not change bad habits.

Capital expenditures will yield a higher return on investment (ROI) when viewed as opportunities to improve patient care and operational efficiency. A willingness to work with consultants or vendors who specialize in process re-engineering and managing change may be necessary where such assistance is needed.

COMMUNICATING VISION AND MANAGING EXPECTATIONS

Any successful EHR implementation begins with the ability to maintain and communicate a clear vision of the goals. Engaging end-users from the outset and maintaining their involvement can positively affect outcomes during actual implementation. Establishing a variety of different means of communication—memos, e-mail, lunch sessions—will ensure full understanding of the project's scope, and will send the dual messages that progress is being made and feedback and suggestions are appreciated. These messages serve to maintain user support. Additionally, if clear and user friendly avenues of communication are opened and publicized early on, end-users should become comfortable with their use and ultimately require less assistance from support staff when system upgrades and enhancements occur.

Excitement and energy will run high in the initial phases of system selection. Although there may be some negativity and resistance, it will likely be subdued by the intensity of the planning activities occurring across the practice.

It is vitally important to identify and manage the expectations derived from the implementation of the EHR. Expectations about the system per se, the pace of the implementation and individual's roles within the organization may be neither clear nor realistic. Common misconceptions during EHR implementations include:

1. The system is so intuitive that any learning curve is minimal.
2. The system is customizable for each user, by each user.

3. Documentation will be accomplished more quickly immediately upon implementation.
4. An EHR "does everything."

Clearly these and any other erroneous impressions must be quickly and publicly (yet patiently and "gently") dispelled.

MANAGING DUAL/MULTIPLE RECORDS

Practices often must face the onerous challenge of maintaining both paper and electronic records. The challenge of maintaining a dual recordkeeping system occurs because paper records still contain important information relevant to the patient. Unless the practice manually enters all past patient information into the EHR, the records for established patients will be incomplete.

Several factors can instigate a dual system of recordkeeping, including a phased-in implementation, limited project scope, having to maintain several sets of medical records, reporting requirements, the scope of data contained in the baseline EHR, and a general hesitation by users to go totally paperless.

Phased-in Implementation

Dual recordkeeping is a by-product of phased-in implementation. If implementation for all clinical aspects of the practice is not executed simultaneously, a clinician may have to go to multiple sources for information necessary to treat the patient. Extra time and effort will be involved in going back and forth between paper and electronic records. This can be ameliorated by scanning paper documents into the EHR system and attaching them as readable files to the patient's electronic record.

Limited Project Scope

Another challenge arises whenever an EHR does not address all the functions required for patient care. For example, a clinical EHR system that does not integrate scheduling or electronic prescribing will require keeping multiple systems, some of them manual.

Dual recordkeeping can also occur when the project scope excludes certain services because of challenges in incorporating the data. For example, digital images from radiology and test results, or electronic prescribing, may not be incorporated in the initial EHR rollout.

Maintaining Several Sets of Medical Records

Dual recordkeeping becomes necessary when the practice maintains several sets of medical records, for example, one set for internal medicine, one for obstetrics/gynecology, one for mental health, and one for social service. Unless these are all incorporated into a single EHR system, the practice will continue to maintain dual record systems.

Reporting Requirements

A functional EHR should be able to extract information from its internal data warehouse and generate reports necessary to comply with public health regulations. Examples of these reports include information vital to communicable disease and immunization registries. The challenge is to negotiate with the health department and other organizations to establish interfaces and accept extracted files that meet the reporting requirement. Receiving the information electronically saves the health department labor costs and thus most will provide assistance in addressing this issue. Once national standards are adopted for transmission of data files, building unique interfaces will no longer be necessary.

Scope of Data Contained in Baseline EHR

The need to maintain dual records may sometimes be necessary at go-live if the information in the EHR is insufficient to adequately understand a patient's health history. If this happens, clinicians will need to access the paper record. As more patient data is entered into the EHR, less time will be spent finding, pulling, and filing charts because the data will be immediately available electronically.

Although time consuming, it may be cost effective to hire temporary clinical staff to enter patient historical data at the beginning of the EHR implementation. Practices might begin by entering information for any patients scheduled for the following week; this method is best for quickly incorporating all the active patients into the EHR system. If time and resources are limited, staff may enter only the pertinent data such as the patient's diagnoses, medications, lab and diagnostic radiology data, drug history and problem list.

Resistance to Change

One of the most important factors leading to the use of dual records, and the most difficult to eradicate, is resistance to change. Clinicians and staff can hesitate to abandon paper simply because they are comfortable with it. However, allowing the practice to maintain dual recordkeeping forces physicians to switch back and forth between the two systems. This impedes workflow, requires staff to spend more time manually entering data from external systems, and increases physicians' resistance to adopting EHR.

Although cumbersome, dual recordkeeping can provide a valuable comparison between the paper-based system and its EHR replacement. When juxtaposed with the often-tedious manual processes required in a paper-based environment, the advantages of the more efficient and complete EHR become evident. In addition, allowing a paper-based backup can allay the fear of potential data loss. Eventually, users will become comfortable with the new technology and wonder what they ever saw in paper-based records.

To complete the transition from paper to digital processing, the practice must evaluate any work processes involving handling paper and how those processes will change once the EHR is implemented. The transition plan should include the following:

1. Identifying what workflows in the office will continue to use paper records and what will transition to the EHR;
2. Educating all staff on where to find information;
3. Understanding how staff will handle the transfer of a patient's record from paper to the EHR; and
4. Training staff to transfer the information.

The negative impact from operating dual systems should be anticipated. The efficiencies inherent in an EHR may not be fully realized during the transition phase. The ROI associated with overhead reduction will also not be realized during the transition. Clinicians and staff, therefore, should not judge the value of the EHR prior to full implementation.

TRANSITION PLAN

The transition plan should clearly identify any risks and define tactical strategies to mitigate those risks. Activities should be clearly identified and linked to specific strategies, necessary changes and priorities, rather than broadly generalized. Milestones should be identified and tied to performance metrics and organizational objectives. Identify how the stakeholders will be affected by each step. Establish communication with all the stakeholders so that each person fully understands his/her role in the implementation and how that role fits into the "big picture."

Contingency plans should be pre-defined yet flexible enough to adjust to unexpected project barriers. Key elements of the transition plan should include the following:

- *Risk identification and prioritization:* Identify actual and potential risks or barriers before and during EHR implementation. When identifying risks, consider:
  - Psychological obstacles (e.g., employee resistance to learning the EHR)
  - Resource obstacles (e.g., does the organization possess adequate staff to complete the implementation?)
  - Technical obstacles (e.g., will the current hardware be sufficient for the new system? Are there any security threats?)

  After being identified, the risks should be ranked according to severity then addressed in order of severity; respond to the most significant risks first.
- *Competing initiatives:* Other projects can compete with an EHR implementation for time, attention or resources. Therefore, do not attempt to manage additional projects such as remodeling the office while implementing an EHR. Resolve competing projects before the implementation begins. An organization that, by necessity, must engage in multiple initiatives should be careful not to divert resources from the EHR implementation.
- *Mitigation strategies:* Try to plan and anticipate the likelihood that a problem will occur. If a problem does occur, this proactive strategy should minimize its negative impact on the EHR implementation.
- *Resource allocation:* In the context of EHR implementation, "resource allocation" will principally refer to whether or not the practice has committed enough of the staff's time to learning and using the EHR.

- *Implementation road map:* The planned steps and strategies in the practice should include a schedule or timeline indicating when each step or milestone should be achieved.

"BIG BANG" VERSUS INCREMENTAL CHANGE

Take "baby steps." The transition from paper to EHR probably should occur incrementally. Each step (segment or module) should be reviewed and analyzed for possible improvement that can be incorporated or applied to future steps.

While an overall plan is required, milestones should be kept small enough to be manageable. Celebrate the attainment of each milestone. Do not wait for the final victory. If individual goals are accomplished, the larger ones will take care of themselves. Keep expectations reasonable and achievable. Achievable goals provide worthy targets, while unreasonable goals breed frustration and are soon discarded.

CHAPTER 14

Phase 7: Training

"A $30,000 electronic medical record system is like a $30,000 grand piano. Whether you play the equivalent of Beethoven's *Moonlight Sonata* or *Chopsticks* depends on your level of training."[23] Sadly, too many practices end up playing *Chopsticks*. In order to successfully implement an EHR system, training must be carefully planned and carried out. If careful analysis is not performed early, the practice will not have a clear vision of exactly what they want the EHR to do for their practice. Most practices try to train everyone quickly while juggling a full load of patients. This will usually "break the piano" and the EHR process will reach an insurmountable roadblock.

Training must begin as early as practical, be continuous, and be readily available throughout the implementation process. As indicated earlier in this book, repeat training should be planned post-implementation to reinforce what has been learned and to account for upgrades in the system and changes in healthcare.

Staff must be willing and capable of being trained. It is vital to have at least some staff who can transition between technical, clinical, and administrative needs. Training for all staff requires that everyone receive instructions appropriate to their job responsibilities.

The training plan must include:

1. The number of hours required for each job position;

2. Resources required for teaching;
3. Appropriate training material;
4. Remedial education related to computers (technology) when required;
5. Uninterrupted scheduling of training; and
6. Enough time to train.

The plan will provide management with an overview of potential disruption to the organization and should anticipate scheduling conflicts. Ideally, temporary employees should be hired as substitutes for permanent staff while they are being trained.

Training may take the form of classroom education, on-the-job experience, self-help and/or written procedures. Most importantly, staff must be freed of their routine duties, and the initial instruction should occur away from the distractions typically present in the office setting.

Consideration may be given to a "train the trainers" program. A "super" user can be trained who will then train everyone else in the practice. Training by internal staff, however, may decrease productivity in a small practice. Usually, an organization must be large enough (e.g., a hospital) to consider internal training.

Post-training proficiency should be monitored and retraining should be available to ensure that clinicians and other staff will use the new system effectively.

SYSTEM TRAINING

Typically, system training is provided by professionals, onsite, who assist staff through the critical early stages of a system startup. Many EHR software products come with extensive online help and other documentation that can be used for tutorial and training purposes. However, most practices will need initial face-to-face training with trainers who are experienced in the system.

System training should be coordinated to occur at proper intervals after software implementation. Formal classroom training early in the implementation is effective in bringing users to a basic level of understanding of the application. More advanced understanding may require on-going onsite instruction.

USER ACCEPTANCE

Staff resistance to training should be evaluated as part of the implementation process. Acceptance testing should be performed in cooperation with the software vendor. In addition, an evaluation should compare the user's responses post-EHR go-live to results from an assessment prior to the EHR. The evaluation should include understanding of both procedures and operational efficiencies.

Training should be available on weekends, after office hours, and during lunchtime. Plan to conduct initial training sessions in classrooms away from the distractions of the workplace. Training should also continue up to the go-live date. This just-in-time, hands-on training will allow users to become more proficient with the EHR system. A mock go-live exercise prior to the actual implementation date can help identify workflows missed during the planning process. In-house or vendor staff should remain on-site for a period of time after go-live to ensure that post-implementation is successful and correct any process errors as soon as they occur.

CHAPTER 15

Phase 8: Go-Live

TIME AND EFFORT TO IMPLEMENT AN EHR

It is no surprise that productivity decreases in the early phases of an EHR implementation. Clinicians and staff will need time to adapt to the new workflow. The learning phase will require time to understand the design and the new processes. In a few weeks, however, the peak of the learning curve will have been reached and productivity will start to increase.

Prior to launch, existing medical record data should be organized in preparation for entry into the new EHR system. New information will need to be entered and integrated with historical information. This effort may challenge the limited resources of an already busy practice but is essential to a smooth transition from a paper to electronic system.

As productivity falls, revenue may be negatively impacted—a financial burden some practices cannot afford. Clinicians who are paid based on productivity may experience a fall in remuneration. Therefore, the budget should include compensation for this period of decreased productivity. This compensation may be paid in cash but other options, such as organizing CME credits for EHR training, may be attractive alternatives.

The fact that physicians and clinics are compensated based on productivity translates to a negative incentive to implement any system that incurs a short-term decrease in efficiency. Therefore, it is important to create incentives so that clinicians and staff embrace the new technology. Some third-party payors are beginning to offer payments similar to bonuses to practices that implement EHR and can demonstrate and measure improved patient care. Measurements may include documentation of an increased number of immunized children, improvement in HEDIS measures such as increased Diabetic HbA1C testing, or an increased number of patients receiving preventive care.

PILOT

To avoid many of the start-up problems discussed above, the practice can start a pilot of the EHR system. The pilot release should utilize the same implementation plan designed for the general release but involve a limited number of clinicians, staff and patients. The selected users should be a good cross sectional sample of the staff, and the pilot should test all functions of the EHR.

This phased-in approach may help identify problems before the real go-live date involving all users and patients. The goal of the pilot is to identify any necessary modifications to the software, hardware, or office workflow.

Once the pilot implementation has been live for a sufficient period of time (at least three to eight weeks), every pilot user should be surveyed to identify any problems that occurred. The survey information should then be reviewed by the entire implementation team and every aspect of the implementation analyzed. Recommendations to resolve issues should be a collective process and the entire team should be empowered to suggest changes.

CONTINGENCY PLANNING

Every project plan incorporates, often tacitly, assumptions related to the project such as time of software and hardware delivery. These assumptions may be beyond the direct control of the project team but are still critical to the success of the project. Therefore it is important to plan for contingencies if the initial plan does not go smoothly.

For example, if the success of the project is dependent on the timely delivery of the software, a mitigating strategy may include inserting a penalty clause in the contract for missing delivery dates. This may help cover some of the income lost as a result of decreased productivity.

EHR implementations frequently involve integration with multiple systems, as well as complex data conversions and migration. It is critical to develop contingency and fall-back plans for each component after go-live. These plans should include capabilities to protect both the hardware system and the data.

"READY, SET, GO-LIVE"

The practice now begins to use the EHR for the entire clinical population. Once go-live occurs, the project manager must monitor software updates, provide users with summaries of those updates, and schedule additional training as necessary.

If the practice selected an EHR that best fits its business structure and workflow, productivity will continue to increase well beyond its level prior to implementation and all the benefits inherent in the system will soon be realized.

CHAPTER 16

Phase 9: Maintenance and Support

MAINTENANCE POST-LIVE ROLLOUT

Both human and financial resources will be required even after the go-live date. Once the EHR has been launched the practice enters the maintenance phase of implementation. Clinical information systems must have a technical foundation that is reliable, high performance, secure, supportable, and adaptable. Therefore, an IT expert must continue to maintain the infrastructure of the computer network. The infrastructure, including servers, operating systems, and/or networks, must be well designed and well maintained. This will require continual monitoring of hardware components and software functionality. In addition, new technology, new regulations, new medical knowledge, and new constructs for the practice of medicine all require continual reassessment and possible modification of the EHR design.

ARRANGING FOR HELP

Most small practices will manage the infrastructure through a service (maintenance) contract with the hardware and/or software vendors. The maintenance agreement should include response to user questions, repairs, outages, site of service, new installation and speed of dispatch to the problem site. The level of service purchased should provide support during, at a minimum, the practice's scheduled hours, but 24/7 level support should be considered. This is especially true if physicians must access the system after hours or on weekends.

PREVENTIVE MAINTENANCE AND DISASTER RECOVERY

Even with the security of a service contract in place, preventive maintenance is required to ensure continuous operation. Daily and routine maintenance should include backing up the data. Ideally, this should be done by the system automatically following office hours. Data should be stored offsite to avoid losing it in a local catastrophe. Power back-up systems are essential in preventing loss of data in the event of electrical outages. The backup should allow the system to power off slowly and automatically save the data before shut-off.

Internet service provider model systems should be maintained and backed up by the vendor through redundant systems that also have dual power supplies. The practice must still oversee the backup and ensure that the vendor continues to provide this service. In the case of regional disasters, an Internet-based system with continuous backup might prevent critical loss of information (e.g., the critical loss that occurred during Hurricane Katrina in 2005).

CONTINUING TO MANAGE CHANGE

The final process in managing change is for the organization to anchor new behavior into its culture.[24] Ongoing resources will have to be made available to ensure that behavioral and cultural changes become permanent. Continual monitoring must be put into place to quickly identify any variation from the initial vision. The organization must remain vigilant to avoid regression and to foster the goals of improved patient care, increased efficiency and decreased liability. These goals must be preserved, reiterated, and re-enforced continually. Deviations that enhance the initial vision, however, should be permitted and discussed.

The practice must hire, promote, and develop employees who enthusiastically endorse change and vision. These employees must ensure that the goals of the project continue to evolve and adapt to future needs of the practice.

CHAPTER 17

Phase 10: Post-Implementation

Maintaining senior level support is as important to post-implementation as it was during the initial stages. Support takes the forms of continued training, responsiveness to staff needs, identification and correction of problems, enhancements to workflow, and ongoing communication.

HIPAA/ACCESS CONTROL

Security and privacy compliance with federal HIPAA regulations are challenging for any medical practice. Many EHR systems, therefore, offer options that can turn the office into a "turn-key" HIPAA-compliant facility. It is difficult to manage the balance between protecting patient information and allowing clinicians to have access to information required for patient care but not everyone in the office needs to have access to that information. Privacy policies are created, therefore, to establish "need to know" categories, and the EHR should be able to both grant and remove user privileges. The system should be able to provide temporary access to non-employees (e.g., third party payors) who have a right to perform chart reviews and all users should be required to sign a statement of compliance with those policies.

EHR systems must also generate an audit trail of any entry into, or change to, the medical record. Random auditing of the system is recommended to help the practice remain HIPAA compliant.

CONTINUOUS IMPROVEMENT

Continuous improvement is the process for achieving incremental improvements in cost, quality, flexibility, delivery speed, and service. To achieve these goals, the practice must continually rethink and redesign its workflow and provide feedback on the results. Implementing an EHR is a continuous process and, once begun, will always need to be monitored for additional improvement.

In order to achieve continuing improvement the practice should do the following:

1. Develop a process for early identification of problems involving all users in resolving those problems.
2. Develop a formal evaluation process and share the results with everyone.
3. Provide feedback and elicit suggestions from staff for continued improvement.
4. Reevaluate strategic decisions to ensure that a consistent business direction is maintained or to justify change in direction.
5. Develop a quality management process that involves everyone in early identification and correction of system flaws.
6. Pilot incremental changes in small groups before releasing the improvements to the rest of the office.
7. Create a mentoring process so clinicians can share their expertise with each other and the rest of the staff.

Hammer and Champy identified the following opportunities for improvement: [25]

- *Combine several jobs into one.* This will reduce labor costs and speed up the improvement process.
- *Let staff make decisions previously made by managers.* This emergent style of change management can result in faster response time and lower cost.
- *Perform process steps in a more natural order.* This will lead to less material handling and improvement in response time.
- *Design more flexible processes.* This will enable staff to more effectively handle contingencies and provide faster turnaround times for the simpler jobs.
- *Perform work where it makes the most sense.* For example, taking blood pressures at a nursing station before the physician sees the patient can improve patient flow through the office.

METRICS

Measuring Attainment of Strategic Goals

Metrics measure the efficacy and progress of the EHR in meeting the business and clinical goals of the practice.

This section will introduce the different types of metrics and define the "balanced scorecard." This approach will help to achieve alignment between the business strategy, technology and organizational factors during EHR implementation.

Types of Metrics

Trends, Targets, Milestones and Benchmarks

Trends indicate the operational efficiency of new processes. They can illustrate improvement, failure, or maintenance of the status quo.

Targets measure attainment of specific goals. They are the end-points of success.

Milestones indicate specific dates for completion of tasks. Names of responsible individuals are often assigned to each milestone so that progress can be tracked.

Benchmarks are used to compare the implemented processes against a corresponding standard. These standards, or best practices, can be measured against competitors locally, regionally, or nationally.

Lead and Lag Indicators

A lead indicator is a metric that indicates, and can even anticipate, successful progress toward EHR implementation and the ROI that comes with it. Lead indicators for a clinical practice typically address cost, efficiency, or use of clinical decision support. For example, a lead indicator for cost might be the time required to bill third party payors or the number of patients who fail to meet requirements for the practice to receive pay for performance bonuses. A typical lead indicator for *efficiency* is the time required to complete a process, for example, generating bills and recording third party payments. A common lead indicator for use of *clinical decision support* is the number of alerts that the system provides to a clinician during the diagnostic evaluation.

A lag indicator is a metric that typically appears after lead indicators. It indicates the degree of completeness or success of the final EHR implementation, or the magnitude of the ROI. Lag indicators do not, however, specify *how* the outcome was achieved, only that it was achieved. Some examples of lag indicators are document management time, patient outcome measurements, medical costs, patient safety, patient satisfaction, access to EHR, efficiency of clinical processes, quality of care, cycle time for lab result turnaround, utilization of EHR by clinicians, and employee satisfaction.

Because these factors indicate the success or failure of EHR implementation, they tend to drive performance.

Criteria for Good Metrics

A good metric must meet the following criteria:

1. It should be strongly correlated with the effect that it is measuring.
2. The metric should measure what is important (and not just what is available). The definitions of what is being measured should be specific and the methods for measuring them should be reproducible. In addition, the data sources should be explicit.
3. The metric should be able to be audited.
4. The metric should be able to measure differences in such parameters as location, shifts, and weekend/weekdays.
5. The cost of measuring the metric should be less than the benefit attained.
6. The metric should have good statistical inference.
7. A decision should be made in advance about who will receive the information measured by the metric. Information given to those who will not benefit from this information is irrelevant.

BALANCED SCORECARD

The balanced scorecard is a framework for measuring and tracking outcome metrics based upon an organization's vision and strategy. The balanced scorecard divides metrics into lead and lag indicators.

The Balanced Scorecard Approach to an EHR Implementation Project

The ultimate goal of an EHR implementation is to reach the targets set in the strategic plan. This plan usually extends over a multi-year period. Its format varies by organization but it always contains information about the current state of the organization, its mission, vision and a plan to achieve that vision. The action plan should contain criteria that will be used to measure the practice's progress toward its strategic goals. Ideally these measurements should be sufficiently detailed as to specify expectations for each employee, and provide reasonable criteria by which to measure progress.

Balanced scorecards consist of a balanced perspective among strategy, finance, customers, business processes, and learning, as shown in Figure 17-1.

Figure 17-1: Balanced Scorecard Perspectives[26]

	Objectives	Measures	Targets	Initiatives
Financial				
Customer				
Process				
Learning				

CHAPTER 18

Factors Driving Success and Failure

DRIVING FORCES

The impetus of implementing an EHR is derived from the perceived gap between the current state of the organization and a desired future state. Furthermore, the impetus is strengthened when the goal of the change is clearly enunciated, and the requirement for change is derived from the use of facts and data.

Effective leadership is essential to ensure that each team member understands his/her role in the process. Tasks must have a person that is responsible for completion, accountable for reporting progress and providing documentation.

RESTRAINING FORCES

Implementation of an EHR sets many restraining forces into motion, including the disruption of existing work patterns, redefinition of workflow, and breakdown of stable power relationships.

Practices planning the organizational changes introduced by an EHR must be prepared to invest management's time and commitment, in addition to financial and human resources. If a practice cannot commit the required resources, the wiser course of action is to delay the implementation.

One of the most significant restraining forces is employee resistance. Hammer and Stanton[27] identify a number of reasons employees resist change, including:

1. Fear of losing job;
2. Loss of power;
3. A lack of skill or knowledge or a resistance to acquire new skills and/or knowledge; and
4. Skepticism about results or benefits of the EHR.

Engaging employees directly in defining and implementing the changes mitigates resistance. Specifically, the following can help:

1. Providing appropriate decisionmaking or approval authority to employees;
2. Allowing employees to develop and use their skills and knowledge to their fullest potential; and
3. Providing the tools, such as technology and training, to enable them to make better decisions.

Risk management is an ongoing process throughout implementation and is the most potent weapon against "restraining forces." Avoidance of risk and plans for mitigation should be incorporated into everyday activities. Restraining forces associated with incomplete design and planning include:

- Lack of cooperation from users and team
- Inappropriate staff assignments
- Divergence of system and business objectives
- Fear of the unknown
- Unacceptably low practice productivity
- Increase in medical errors
- Budget overruns
- System may not fulfill intended use
- Customization could become costly or increase project scope
- Processing policies and procedures may not be practical
- Position (job) descriptions may not match assigned responsibilities
- System may be vulnerable to unauthorized use
- System may not perform as anticipated
- System (potential) instability

- Interfaces may not accommodate data requirements
- Conversion of data from previous systems may not map to new system
- User training may not be appropriate or complete
- Hardware, software, or network failures
- Insufficient equipment to accomplish task
- Insufficient personnel to accomplish tasks
- Organization not prepared to accommodate new system
- Site not ready for users or new IT equipment

While many of the preceding restraints may be temporary and most are not devastating, left unmitigated, many would cause severe organizational pain and might eventually result in poor patient care and/or business failure.

FACTORS FOR SUCCESSFUL EHR IMPLEMENTATION

The following summary for successful EHR implementations appears in a recent white paper:[28]

Critical Success Factors:
1. Select the right internal leadership team.
2. Communicate the "what's in it for me?" to obtain buy-in from all users.
3. Analyze the current office workflow (i.e., how things are done).
4. Create specific and measurable goals.
5. Develop a strategy for entering existing data.
6. Devote sufficient time to training.
7. Plan to create power users or super users who can help others.
8. Create an ongoing plan for answering questions.
9. Leave time buffers throughout the day.
10. Plan to succeed, and you will.

Mitigating Pitfalls:
- *Selection*: appropriate analysis of available EHRs takes time and skill
- *Negotiation*: experience helps
- *Documentation*: can never have enough
- *Hardware*: lack of standards supports reliability is expensive in the long run

Mitigating Success Factors:
- Clinicians investing their time at appropriate phases of the process
- Staff buy-in and collaboration from the outset, so they are eager to use the system
- Accurate analysis of clinical and business needs to deliver the best solution
- Implementing in stages, hence gaining incremental benefits
- Effective training, start-up continuous support
- Willingness to invest the effort to master and incorporate into the practice the tools an EHR provides

Employing External Consultants:
- Works on behalf of the practice and not for the vendor
- Manages the initiative and decision making process from experience
- Maximizes the use of staff time
- Matches best-fit technology to each person's work styles and business needs
- Applies usability and process improvement expertise
- Cost for service ends with completion of project

PRINCIPLES OF SUCCESSFUL PROJECTS

Project organization and adequate staffing are also critical to success. Bing describes various "Principles of Successful Projects" based on his extensive practical experience in the field.[29] These principles include the following:

1. There must be a single leader (project manager) who is experienced and willing to take the responsibility for the work.
2. There must be an informed and supportive management that delegates appropriate authority to the project manager.
3. There must be a dedicated team of qualified people to do the work of the project.
4. The project goal must be clearly defined along with priorities of the shareholders or stakeholders.
5. There must be an integrated plan that outlines the action required in order to reach the goal.
6. There must be a schedule establishing the time goals of the project.
7. There must be a budget of costs and/or resources required for the project.

All stakeholders must be brought into the planning process early in order to consider and plan for the temporary impact on work processes (flow).

EIGHT REASONS FOR FAILURE

In accordance with Chin's findings, Lorenzi and Riley summarize eight main reasons for system implementation *failures*: [20]

1. *Communication failure:* caused by ineffective listening and failure to prepare the staff for a new system.
2. *Cultural change failure:* caused by unwillingness to accept impending change. Strategies should be incorporated to nurture a positive culture or to grow a new one.
3. *Complexity failure:* caused by underestimating the complexity of the project resulting in loss of credibility.
4. *Scope creep failure:* caused by unrealistic expectations of the system. To counteract scope creep, the criteria for success must be clearly identified "up front."
5. *Organizational failure:* caused by a lack of clear vision of change, a lack of empowerment and ability (including power/authority) to act upon problems, a lack of support by upper management, lack of resources, and an inability to measure success.
6. *Technology failure:* caused by inadequate testing and/or a system that is too technical to understand.
7. *Training failure:* caused by poor training, bad timing of training, or an inappropriate level of training.
8. *Leadership failure:* caused by a lack of commitment on the part of the leader, overextension of his/her time, delegation without supervision, no "ownership" of the effort, poor political skills, and over-statement of products features to get approval (the "easy, cheap, or perfect" solution).

Lorenzi and Riley also identified some practical applications of change management that can enhance the ability of the modern organization to adapt to change, stating that "creating change starts with creating a vision for change and empowering individuals to act as change agents to attain that vision."[20]

For example, resistance to the change from paper-based documentation to an EHR may result when users attempt to incorporate a new workflow into their day, but cannot translate the old paper based method to the new electronic system. By recognizing and addressing such problems early in the design phase of the project, successful buy-in and implementation can occur.

Hence, the project manager in an ambulatory healthcare office must recognize that the operational changes inherent in implementing an EHR may seriously impact the way that different end-users perform their jobs. This critical change must be strategically planned and managed, and the solution must meet the needs of the medical office.

In summary, major challenges to successful EHR implementations are often more behavioral than technical. Thus, the implementation champion must recognize the importance of behavioral change. Resistance to change is a common and ongoing problem that requires knowledge of the complex system of relationships between people, leaders, technologies, and work processes.[20] Managing change and human factors throughout the EHR implementation process will help ensure success. This will result in clinician satisfaction and efficiency, well-targeted functionality, and clinical content that remain up-to-date and relevant to the unique needs of each EHR implementation setting.

CHAPTER 19

A View from the Trenches

EHR IMPLEMENTATION IN SMALL, PRIVATE PRACTICE SETTINGS

In October 2004 this author* implemented a demonstration pilot project for EHR implementation. Fifteen medical offices deemed by this author to be most likely to accept an EHR were canvassed for their participation.

Of the 15 offices, only 5 agreed to become part of the project, with the rest citing inability to afford the required hardware for the project. In most cases the hardware costs ranged between $15,000 and $35,000 depending upon the size of the practice and number of work stations required. Therefore, the barrier of cost remained an obstacle for the small group medical practice.

Another barrier was the lack of familiarity of some of the practices with EHRs in general. In addition, this author could not find an EHR champion at any of the offices who chose not to participate. Among those who did, a lack of staff resources obligated the physician to become both the EHR champion and the individual with the power to delegate tasks for EHR implementation.

*Steven Arnold, MD.

Most of the offices that agreed to be part of the pilot were not well organized. They had little to no defined goals for their practices other than to become more efficient. There was no clearly stated or understood business mission and no concept of strategic advantage or sustainable competitive edge.

Although the majority of physicians in these practices communicate well with their patients, they were poor communicators within their business microcosm. As a result of not being able to articulate the vision for EHR in their practices, some physician leaders were unable to achieve buy-in from the staff.

The implementation team consisted of three individuals under the employ of the EHR vendor chosen for this project. The team consisted of one trainer, one programmer, and one computer engineer. Their assignment was to install the hardware and software, program any final changes to adjust to the varied needs of the different practices, and then train the physician(s) and their staff.

CASE 1: SOME PRACTICES NEVER GET OFF THE GROUND

Setting: Private ambulatory care practice with three physicians, an office manager, a billing person, and five ancillary staff (no lab technicians).

Prior to their arrival the implementation team coordinated the details of the project plan with Dr. W, the senior physician and decisionmaker for the practice. The plan included where to set up the hardware, when to train the staff, and a tentative implementation schedule. Dr. W assured the team that he understood (a) the purpose of the EHR; (b) what the implementation entailed; (c) his role as champion and senior decisionmaker; and (d) his business goals (to improve quality and efficiency in the office). The team took him at his word and did not test his comprehension of the plan and design; this proved to be a mistake.

The implementation team arrived at the office after office hours on the first day to install the hardware. The first problem encountered was that, although agreed to in the initial design, Dr. W failed to install an ethernet to handle broadband transmission of data.

The team installed the hardware and returned the next day for training. However, Dr. W was not present. Instead, the team was greeted by the office manager who was somewhat surprised by the sudden appearance of all the equipment. Dr. W had not apprised any of the staff of his intentions to implement an EHR, with the exception of vague plans he shared only with the office manager.

Dr. W was not easily reached throughout the implementation and seldom came to the office. The office manager, however, was able to assist in planning how the EHR would be integrated. Given that Dr. W had not informed the staff of the change, the office manager assumed the role of the EHR champion and the implementation team assumed the responsibility of introducing the EHR to the staff. They were able to achieve buy-in with two of the staff who were excited by the advent of technology into the office. The majority of the staff, however, were resistant. The billing person, who had the most power in the office after the physicians and office manager, balked at the implementation. She remarked that it would occur "over my dead body" and was obviously concerned that the billing portion of the EHR might supplant her power or, worse, her job. All of the staff were concerned over not having been informed by Dr. W of this project.

Dr. W, who had championed and coordinated the EHR initiative, was present less than any of his staff throughout the implementation. Although the team was able to motivate the office manager and some of the staff to learn and to use the EHR, the team did not have either legitimate or expert power in the office and could not change behavior, culture, or compel the staff to fully cooperate. There was a lack of understanding of the technology, skills, training, and work effort required to run this project. Dr. W never took the time to fully understand the project and, thus, underestimated its complexity.

Dr. W decided that he would not learn the EHR system until his staff was adequately trained. He failed to create an incentive program to reward the staff for the extra time they needed to spend on this project. As a result the staff was not motivated to use the EHR and viewed senior management (Dr. W) as being nonsupportive.

Dr. W continued to be absent from training and did not make time to work with the team to customize the disease management templates and preferred drugs/diagnoses/procedures databases. Without his leadership the billing manager continued to refuse to use the program and one of the other physicians declined to learn the system if Dr. W was not making the effort to learn it.

Workflow design was hampered by the staff's inability to answer simple questions about how patients traversed the office during a medical visit. The scheduling component of the EHR was delayed due to the inconsistent work hours for the physicians.

Follow-up

The implementation team returned several times over the next six months to try to revive the implementation. Training sessions were scheduled via phone, but neither Dr. W nor any of his staff kept the appointments. Six months after the installation, the office manager quit and the EHR implementation came to an abrupt ending.

One year later Dr. W had a demonstration of the EHR system that was working smoothly and effectively in another office. He has since contacted the "Dr. Know" implementation team and asked to re-start the process.

Discussion

The problems encountered with this practice's implementation were largely the result of failure to identify an EHR champion and lack of top management commitment and support. Even if Dr. W had delegated the role of EHR champion to another willing individual, his office manager, his lack of commitment would still have derailed the process. More detrimental to the implementation than the lack of a champion is a declared champion who is absent, incapable or disinterested.

In addition to failure in leadership, other reasons cited for the problems in Dr. W's office included a failure in communication, Dr. W's underestimation of the complexity of the implementation and the EHR system itself, unwillingness of at least one employee to change behavior or culture and a dysfunction in the organization of the office itself.

Also working against a successful implementation were a lack of a clearly defined business goal, a lack of qualified personnel with the skills necessary to run the EHR system, no clearly defined goal with time lines and milestones, and very little understanding of who the stakeholders were and what needs had to be addressed.

CASE 2: SOME TAKE SHORT HOPS DOWN THE RUNWAY

Setting: Private ambulatory care practice with three physicians and three ancillary staff (including one lab technician).

Dr. X had consulted with his two colleague physicians about whether to purchase an EHR. At the time, the practice relied exclusively on paper-based processes and outsourced billing. Recognizing the need to modernize, the two physicians supported Dr. X's idea. Dr. X took the initiative to acquire an EHR and arrange for its implementation.

Dr. X's practice functioned better than Dr. W's practice even though they had no office manager; Dr. X functioned in that role. The doctors had discussed the implementation with their staff and prepared them psychologically for the change. Dr. X's staff was amenable and responsive to the need for change and there was no obvious resistance. Unlike Dr. W's staff, Dr. X's staff had a better understanding of, and control over, the workflow. Moreover, they were cognizant of their doctors' schedules and knew where they were at all times.

Dr. X assumed the role of champion as an extension of his leadership in coordinating the EHR effort. He was the logical choice because (a) he was most familiar with the EHR, and (b) there were no other management-level personnel to assume the champion role. The other two doctors were reluctant to lead the process.

Before implementation Dr. X assured the implementation team that he understood the EHR concept and needed only to learn how it worked. The team made another mistake in not testing the EHR champion's true knowledge of the system. Dr. X missed the point that an EHR's purpose is not to electronically replicate paper-based charting but to evolve the practice's workflow and enable doctors to provide higher quality care. He insisted that all paper records be scanned into the EHR prior to the go-live date. The implementation team disagreed, contending that, although valuable, scanning was a distraction to setting up the EHR. Scanning charts before going live is counter-productive because information will still have to be added to paper charts until the go-live milestone is reached. This results in generation of extra work through duplication of efforts. Waiting to scan charts until after going live eliminates much of the duplication and also affords the staff more time to learn the EHR.

Like Dr. W, Dr. X was not an effective EHR champion. Although he demonstrated senior management support and was a tireless advocate of EHR, he did not have time to learn about or oversee the process. His 12-hour days were split between his office and hospital practices. Because he was away from his office so often, his staff strayed in their commitment to the implementation.

The transition to EHR was difficult for the staff because they had never used computers. Their lack of skills slowed training. Compounding this problem was the fact that some of the staff were recent immigrants to America and, although they communicated easily with Spanish-speaking patients, they were not fluent in English. Moreover, Dr. X did not reduce the staff's workload, thereby encroaching on their time to learn the EHR. Eventually, out of frustration, the staff gradually reverted to the "old way" of doing things.

Through communication with the implementation team Dr. X agreed to hire someone with computer experience to help spearhead the EHR effort. He delegated his champion role to this new employee, thereby giving the employee legitimate power in the office.

The implementation team trained the staff and the new employee and planned to return to train the doctors once the patient demographics were entered and staff became more proficient at using the EHR.

Follow-up

The new employee, initially dedicated to the EHR implementation, was gradually assigned to helping the overworked staff with their roles. This resulted in sporadic use of the EHR system and the staff stopped using it within the first few months. Dr. X then refocused the EHR-dedicated employee, who retrained the staff. EHR implementation was completed within the next three months and the office has utilized the system effectively since.

Discussion

Although Dr. X was committed to the EHR project and was involved in the design phase of the implementation, his responsibilities soon took him away from the implementation process. His leadership of the project failed. The original plan, well-designed and integrated, was disrupted. Project time lines and milestones were ignored. As a result, organization and behavioral changes necessary to complete a successful implementation were halted. Dr. X committed further resources to the project and delegated his leadership to an appropriate individual. However, the new skilled resources were soon displaced due to Dr. X's inability to accept the initial short-term decrease in productivity. Fortunately, Dr. X's commitment never diminished and he was able to accept the loss in productivity and demonstrated the leadership necessary to get the project back on track.

CASE 3: SOME ASCEND A FEW FEET

Setting: Private ambulatory care practice with three physicians, an office manager, two billing people, and 15 ancillary staff (including three lab technicians).

Dr. Y's motivation to implement an EHR system was initiated by his failure to pass the health plan's quality chart reviews. Although Dr. Y was open-minded about using an EHR, the health plan forced the issue by threatening to terminate him from their network unless he implemented an EHR system. His motivation was thus external and punitive. Dr. Y had very little intrinsic motivation to implement an EHR system.

The implementation team found Dr. Y's understanding of EHR to be unrealistic; he felt that an electronic system would "magically" solve his problems with the health plan.

Dr. Y became involved in the design and implementation roadmap. He dictated that the physicians would be fully trained once patient demographics were loaded into the system and the staff became proficient at using it.

He assumed the role of EHR champion and project leader. He informed his staff about the EHR prior to its implementation and appropriately reduced their workload so they could focus on learning the system. He hired two additional employees during implementation to facilitate the transition, encouraged the staff to begin using the program immediately, and committed himself to working with the implementation team to tailor the EHR to his practice.

Although the implementation got off to a good start, it soon reached an impasse. Dr. Y was a multi-tasker who found it difficult to concentrate totally on one project at a time. Although he was a micro-manager, he was disorganized and spontaneous. He often changed workflows and procedures abruptly and, sometimes, at whim. As a result his office staff became confused and workflow was frequently disrupted. Dr. Y frequently disrupted his own training to attend to other matters such as seeing an unscheduled patient or answering phone calls.

To alleviate this problem the implementation team scheduled training times for Dr. Y during hours when he was least likely to be disturbed. It soon became apparent, however, that Dr. Y had little understanding of how to align the EHR with his business needs and goals. He saw the EHR only as an electronic means of making his current system more efficient. Unfortunately, Dr. Y was unable to accept the fact that his current system was dysfunctional. It soon became evident that he did not want to alter or improve his workflow or delivery of quality patient care. He was merely implementing the EHR as a way to appease the health plan. Because Dr. Y never internalized his motivation to implement an EHR, his commitment soon waned. It became apparent that, under his direction, the EHR project was unsustainable.

The other two physicians in the practice had initial training to use the EHR and the nurses, who had been fully trained, stood ready to enter the appropriate patient information. Unfortunately, Dr. Y would not allow the other physicians to use the EHR before he learned the system. Therefore, the implementation team was not permitted to continue to train them.

Dr. Y's micro-management style also halted implementation of the EHR billing module; the billing manager was not permitted to use the program until Dr. Y was confident that he had mastered it himself. As a result, the billing manager became disinterested and suspected that the implementation would not continue. Two of Dr. Y's staff also resigned from the practice during this time and the implementation came to a halt until the staff was replaced 30 days later.

Follow-up

The implementation team made several more attempts to teach Dr. Y but he was unable to concentrate for any extended length of time. He also had forgotten most of what he had been taught on prior occasions. The team suspected that Dr. Y suffered from "adult attention deficit disorder."

Despite the barriers, the EHR began to take root. The receptionists found the scheduling module to be superior to anything they had used before. Despite Dr. Y's insistence that he be trained first, the billing manager began to use the billing module. Dr. Y eventually acquiesced to the billing manager's desire to use the system and the billing module was implemented successfully.

Discussion

The major obstacle to EHR implementation in this setting was that the EHR champion became the champion for the wrong reasons. Dr. Y was driven by extrinsic motivation that was not sustainable. He did not integrate the EHR design into his business goals and he was resistant to changes in the workflow to accommodate the EHR.

Although he communicated well to his staff, his distractions and abrupt style of leadership (authoritarian in a setting where the staff would have benefited from a permissive style) led to confusion and organizational failure. Training failed because Dr. Y insisted on learning the EHR himself before anyone else, yet he was the most difficult of all to train.

Fortunately, the enthusiasm of his staff allowed the implementation to proceed. Once the employees who had resigned were replaced, the staff settled down and began to recognize the benefits of an EHR. As a result, they internalized the EHR concept. In the absence of clear direction from senior management (Dr. Y) the staff became a collective champion and began to change the culture in the office by modifying their behavior.

CASE 4: SOME TAKE OFF COMPLETELY

Setting: Private ambulatory care practice with two physicians, an office manager, a billing person, and five ancillary staff (including three lab technicians).

Dr. Z was unlike the other physicians. Dr. Z had been interested in EHRs for at least six months before becoming part of the "Dr. Know" Beta project but was unable to purchase one due to budgetary constraints. A stipend from the health plan to help defray the cost of hardware enabled Dr. Z to move forward. He compared numerous EHR systems and then carefully reviewed his office workflow and business practices. He anticipated a short-term reduction in productivity as a result of EHR implementation and had prepared his staff for the changes in workflow that would occur.

Dr. Z was, at the same time, the EHR champion and senior management supporter for the practice. He did not underestimate the complexity of the implementation process and committed his time to the training. He encouraged his staff to do the same. In contrast to Dr. Z, however, the staff was ambivalent about implementing an EHR system in the office. There were some skills, however, that were already present before the implementation began. The staff had used computers to check patient eligibility online but the EHR, by comparison, was far more complex and they were afraid of the disruption it might bring to the office.

With this ambivalence in mind, the implementation team took small, calculated steps in training the staff. They began by using the familiar Internet through the EHR system. As the staff grew more comfortable navigating simpler parts of the EHR they became motivated to further their learning. With Dr. Z's enthusiasm motivating them the staff quickly adapted to the full EHR functionality.

Dr. Z began using the EHR as soon as he was trained. Almost immediately, he began crafting his disease management templates. He selected his favorite drug prescriptions, diagnoses, and procedures and took other actions to customize the EHR to his practice.

Dr. Z's routine use of the EHR helped him retain what he learned during training and helped him elucidate how the functions of the EHR corresponded to his current workflow. He was able to rethink and improve his clinical and business processes. Thus, not only was the EHR aligned with his business processes, it created a milieu in which those processes could be observed and improved.

To speed the process of implementation, the team was able to extract patient demographic information from Dr. Z's billing package and import them into the EHR. This saved a significant amount of the staff's time and enabled them to use the EHR to see patients almost immediately. Therefore, the disruption of workflow in the early stages of implementation was negligible.

Follow-up

Six months after implementation Dr. Z and his staff continue to successfully use the entire EHR system including the clinical, scheduling, billing, and prescribing modules. Dr. Z has been able to identify patients who need preventive care, treatment, or follow-up and who would have been missed through the manual system. His patient flow increased by 20% and his income by 15% (this difference between volume and income is explained by the number of capitated patients for whom Dr. Z did not receive any additional income).

Discussion

Dr. Z's success was the result of clearly defined goals and his ability to become both the EHR champion and project leader. He communicated well with his staff and allowed them enough time to train. Their initial resistance was greatly diminished by his senior level support and enthusiasm for the project.

Dr. Z had anticipated a slow down in workflow but this was ameliorated by the ability to electronically transfer patient demographics from his billing into the EHR system. His staff's limited computer skills facilitated EHR training during implementation and enabled them to learn the system quickly.

Dr. Z was cognizant of the needs of the health plan in terms of delivery of quality care and preventive medicine. He gradually initiated a cultural change in the office but was not limited by a disorganization seen in the other Beta site offices.

In general, this was the ideal situation, and the EHR implementation was a complete success.

FURTHER DISCUSSION

Understanding the Goals

Don't implement until the champion truly understands his/her goals. Often, physicians who serve as EHR champions possess only a nebulous idea of what they want. They may never get beyond the desire to increase office efficiency but must understand that the early phases of implementation can, and will, temporarily slow productivity.

Don't think for the physician. A vendor should assist physicians in defining their objectives for an EHR, but often the vendor defines the goals for the physician. A physician who does not think diligently about an EHR is unlikely to possess any intrinsic motivation toward its adoption. Goals suggested by the vendor are not enough in ensuring a successful implementation.

Milestones must be managed. It is the responsibility of the project leader to manage milestones. In many cases this individual is also the EHR champion. The vendor can assist the project leader but should not assume this responsibility unless the office is so small that outsourcing these activities becomes critical to the overall success of the EHR implementation.

Skill barriers. Many physicians and staff lack basic computer skills necessary to use an EHR. In that case, physicians and staff should learn the basic skills before implementation, or allow more time during implementation for training.

Language barriers. If the physicians or staff do not speak English as a first language (or their first language is not the same as the trainers'), allow more time for the implementation or, if necessary, hire a translator. English was not the native language of some of the staff in Case 2, so concepts took somewhat longer to convey than in other offices.

On-site experience. Implementations proceed more smoothly when someone in the office is familiar with computers. This person need not be a computer expert but should have enough experience to perform simple tasks such as changing printer toner or downloading a file. Although larger institutions often have resident IT staff, this is rare in small practices. The practices in Cases 3 and 4 each had at least one individual knowledgeable about computers. In both instances the offices learned and adopted the EHR more quickly.

Staff turnover. A high turnover in staff greatly slows implementation and can sidetrack it completely. During the pilot implementations, many of Dr. Y's staff quit because of dissatisfaction with the office management. As a result, the implementation stopped while the remaining staff took on the former employees' responsibilities.

Unrealistic expectations. A surprising number of people who purchase EHRs do not actually understand what the EHR does. During the pilot implementation, for example, physicians frequently requested that all their paper records be immediately scanned into the computer system. While the virtues of this are debatable, the reason doctors requested that the charts be scanned was extremely revealing. They were under the impression that upon scanning a chart into an EHR, the EHR could read the chart—even if handwritten—and then move the medical data into the appropriate areas of the EHR. Moreover, they expected this scanned information to be searchable. Such technology does not exist.

Scope creep. Beware of scope creep when physicians and staff view the EHR as an electronic tool capable of doing everything. It is vital that the practice continue to use the project plan as its roadmap. The scope of the EHR must always remain clearly defined from the design phase to go-live. In other words, "stick to the plan."

References

1. American Medical Association. *Physician Master File.* December, 2000.

2. Reed M, Grossman J. Limited information technology for patient care in physician offices. Center for Studying Health System Change, Issue Brief No. 89, September, 2004. Available at www.hschange.org/CONTENT/708/. Accessed June 30, 2006.

3. Harris Interactive. Canada and U.S. trail other countries in use of EMR and electronic prescribing. Available at www.pdacortex.com/harris_emr.htm. Accessed June 30, 2006.

4. CDC Report. Use of computerized clinical support systems in medical settings: United States, 2001-2003. August, 2005.

5. U.S. Dept of Labor, Bureau of Labor Statistics. Available at www.bls.gov. Accessed June 30, 2006.

6. Markle Foundation. Achieving electronic connectivity in healthcare. July, 2004. Available at www.connectingforhealth.org/resources/cfh_aech_roadmap_072004.pdf. Accessed June 30, 2006.

7. May L. Major causes of software project failures. *Cross Talk.* July, 1998. Available at www.stsc.hill.af.mil/crosstalk/1998/07/causes.asp. Accessed June 30, 2006.

8. Brailer D. ONCHIT Executive Summary 2004. Available at www.hhs.gov/onchit/framework/hitframework/executivesummary.html. Accessed December 3, 2005.

9. Beckman Coulter Online Reports. U.S. healthcare costs increase for sixth consecutive year. Available at www.beckman.com/resourcecenter/diagtoday/articles/features/healthcarecostsincrease.asp. Accessed June 30, 2006.

10. Rand Research Brief. Health information technology: Can HIT lower costs and improve quality? RB9136-Health, 2005. Rand Corporation.

11. American Diabetes Association. Economic costs of diabetes in the U.S. in 2002. *Diabetes Care.* 2003; 26:917-932.

12. Kennedy P. The best healthcare system in the world. Remarks of Cong. Patrick J. Kennedy presented at the 2004 Annual HIMSS Conference & Exhibition; February 26, 2004.

13. Frisch B, Gallagher T, Woodson B. National trends in healthcare consumerism: The influential healthcare consumer. Second Annual Report from Solucient, LLC, August, 2003. Available at www.solucient.com/docs/NationalTrends082503.pdf. Accessed December 3, 2005.

14. Harris Interactive. How the public sees health records and an EMR program. Study No. 23283, February, 2005.

15. Bennis W, Benne K, Chin R. *The Planning of Change.* 2nd ed. New York: Holt, Rinehart and Winston; 1969.

16. Markle Foundation. Achieving electronic connectivity in healthcare. July 2004. Available at www.connectingforhealth.org/resources/cfh_aech_roadmap_072004.pdf. Accessed June 30, 2006.

17. Glaser J. Lessons learned: implementing a clinical information system can offer a rich education. *Healthcare Informatics.* September, 2002.

18. Aarts J, Doorewaard H, Berg M. Understanding implementation: The case of a computerized physician order entry system in a large Dutch university medical center. *J Amer Med Inform Assoc.* 2004; 11:207-216.

19. Chin R. The reality of EHR implementation: Lessons from the field. *The Economist.* April 15, 2004.

20. Lorenzi N, Riley R. Knowledge and change in health care organizations. *Stud Health Technol Inform.* 2000; 76:63-69.

21. Kubler Ross J. *On Death and Dying.* New York: Touchstone; 1969.

22. Blattner S, Wenneker M. Getting physician buy-in: Even without direct authority. *The Physician Executive.* September-October, 2005.

23. Lowes R. EHR success: Training is the key. *The Connected Physician.* May 7, 2004.

24. Kotter J. Leading Change. Library of Congress; 1996.

25. Hammer M, Champy J. *Reengineering the Corporation: A Manifesto for Business Revolution.* London: HarperCollins; 1993.

26. Kaplan RS, Norton DP. The balanced scorecard: Translating strategy into action. Available at www.quickmba.com/accounting/mgmt/balanced-scorecard/. Accessed December 3, 2005.

27. Hammer M, Stanton S. *The Reengineering Revolution*. New York: Harper Business; 1994.

28. Misys Healthcare Systems. Critical Success Factors for Practice-Wide EHR Implementations (white paper).

29. Bing J. Principles of project management. PMNETwork, PMI. January, 1994, p. 40.

Further Reading on Change Management

Implementing an EHR results in massive changes on both the organizational and the individual level. No discussion of EHR implementation is complete without including the topic of change management. A wealth of information and theory exists about managing the process of organizational change and how employees at all levels of the organization maneuver through and hopefully adapt to the change. Some of the more prominent works in the field include the following:

- **Bennis W, Benne K, Chin R. *The Planning of Change*, Second Edition. New York: Holt, Rinehart and Winston; 1969.** The authors offer four basic human behavioral characteristics, whether or not people are (a) perceived as rational and open; (b) willing to accept to different cultural norms and values; (c) compliant and willing to adhere to authority; or (d) adaptive to new circumstances after loss or disruption.

- **Deutsch M, Krauss R. *Theories in Social Psychology*. New York: Basic Books; 1965.** The authors discuss Kurt Levin's work in psychology and sociology and credit him with creating the field theory in social psychology. They summarize Lewin's work as focusing on the individual's motivation to resolve tension when faced with either conflict between two equally positive goals or two equally negative goals, or opposing positive and negative forces.

- **Lippitt GL. *Visualizing Change.* Fairfax: NTL Learning Resources Corporation; 1973.** Lippitt modifies Lewin's work and discusses several phases of planned change that include (a) achieving a clear diagnosis of the problem; (b) assessment of motivation and ability to change; (c) involvement of a "change agent" in an appropriate role (and the extent of that agent's motivation and resources); (d) creating clear and progressive objectives; and (e) maintaining the change with the ultimate goal being to dissolve the role of the change agent.

- **Cotter JJ. *The 20% Solution: Using Rapid Redesign to Create Tomorrow's Organizations Today.* ISBN: 0-471-13278-0, Nov 1995.** Cotter discusses change in terms of personal loss by the individual and suggests a number of ways organizations can deal with resistance to change by developing a "check list for success" for their implementations.

- **Prochaska JO, DiClemente CC, Norcross JC. In search of how people change: Applications to addictive behaviors. *American Psychologist.* 1992; 47.** The Stages of Change Model, introduced by Prochaska and DiClemente, evolved from work with smoking cessation and the treatment of drug and alcohol addiction. In this model, behavioral change is viewed in five distinct stages of readiness: (a) lack of awareness of the need for change; (b) contemplating change; (c) reaching a decision to change; (d) acting on the decision; and (e) maintaining the achieved change over time through the use of aids and reminders. Attempts to influence an individual to change are more likely to succeed when the message is tailored to his or her stage of readiness.

- **Bridges W, Mitchell S. Leading transition: A new model for change. *Leader to Leader.* 2000; 16:30-36.** Bridges and Mitchell offer the concept of transition as an internal state through which people must progress in order for change (which is viewed as an external event) to be successful.

- **Rogers EM. *Diffusion of Innovation.* Fifth Edition. New York: Free Press; 2003.** Roger researched how new ideas (innovations) are adopted by organizations. He divided the adoption process into two sub-processes: initiation and implementation. Initiation includes information gathering, conceptualizing, and planning for the adoption of the innovation. Implementation includes the events, actions, and decisions involved with utilizing the innovation. He identified that the discrepancy between the organization's actual performance and its expectations, identified as a "performance gap," initiates the innovation process. An important point identified by Rogers is that both the "innovation and organization change during the innovation process" (p. 434). The ability to redefine and restructure the innovation to fit the needs of the organization and the widespread use and understanding of the innovation are crucial elements for the long-term sustainability of the organizational change.

Index